PEOPLE AND PLACES

PEOPLE AND PLACES

An East Anglian Miscellany

TRUMPINGTON: A Cambridgeshire Village
by Edith Carr

A WHEELWRIGHT OF HOXNE: A Story of Country Life
by Betty Rutterford

CULFORD HALL: near Bury St Edmunds
by Gertrude Storey

TERENCE DALTON LIMITED
LAVENHAM . SUFFOLK
1973

Published by
TERENCE DALTON LIMITED
SBN 900963 24 7

Printed in Great Britain at
The Lavenham Press Limited
Lavenham   Suffolk

Contents

Index of Illustrations 6

TRUMPINGTON: A Cambridgeshire Village

Chapter 1	The Manors	10
Chapter 2	Justice	18
Chapter 3	Mediaeval Times	23
Chapter 4	The Parish	30
Chapter 5	The People	35
Chapter 6	From Elizabeth to James II	40
Chapter 7	Village Life	50
Chapter 8	The Changing Times	57
Chapter 9	And Then Victoria	63
Authorities Consulted	67
Photograph Acknowledgements	67

A WHEELWRIGHT OF HOXNE: A Story of Country Life 69

CULFORD HALL: near Bury St Edmunds

Introduction	94
Chapter 1	The Beginnings	96
Chapter 2	Rectors of Culford and Parishioners in the Fourteenth and Fifteenth Centuries ..	101
Chapter 3	The Bacons of Culford	108
Chapter 4	Lady Jane	113
Chapter 5	Sir Frederick Cornwallis	127
Chapter 6	A New Chapter	141
Chapter 7	Quiet Interlude	147
Chapter 8	The Marquisate 1762-1823	153
Chapter 9	The New Village	167
Chapter 10	"Qui Invidet Minor Est"	174
Chapter 11	The Church of St Mary, Culford	185
Conclusion	197
Bibliography	199
Acknowledgements	200

Index of Illustrations

TRUMPINGTON

(i)   The old Mill at Trumpington.
(ii)   Trumpington Church in 1842.
(iii)   Sir Roger de Trumpington, died 1289.
(iv)   Shepherd and sheep near the river in the 1870s.
(v)   The A10 Cambridge to Royston road.
(vi)   The blacksmith's forge about 1880.
(vii)   The blacksmith's forge in 1945.
(viii)   Trumpington men of the 'eighties.
(ix)   The *Tally Ho* inn about 1905.
(x)   The High Street, Trumpington, 1923.
(xi)   The old *Red Lion* in the 1920s.
(xii)   Whitlock's Almshouses.
(xiii)   Trumpington Hall.
(xiv)   Wash day in the 1900s.
(xv)   War Memorial in 1921.

A WHEELWRIGHT OF HOXNE

(i)   Aubrey Leggett during the First World War.
(ii)   Una Green, née Leggett, during the First World War.
(iii)   Family Group.
(iv)   Aubrey Leggett in 1957.
(v)   Hoxne school photograph 1900.
(vi)   Herbert Leggett at his wheelwright's shop.
(vii)   The old *Red Lion,* Hoxne.
(viii)   Low Street, Hoxne, before the First World War.
(ix)   Aubrey and Una Leggett, 1902.
(x)   David Leggett.
(xi)   Caravans made by Aubrey Leggett.
(xii)   Chair-o-planes at Hoxne.
(xiii)   Lychgate at Hoxne Church.

CULFORD HALL

(i)   The first Culford Hall.
(ii)   Culford Hall after alterations.
(iii)   North face of the Hall today.
(iv)   South face of the Hall today.
(v)   Main staircase.
(vi)   Plan of alterations to Hall.
(vii)   The lake at Culford Hall.
(viii)   Stone bridge at Culford Hall.
(ix)   Sir Nathaniel Bacon.
(x)   First Marquis Cornwallis.
(xi)   Marlborough and Cadogan, Malplaquet.
(xii)   Tomb of Lady Jane Bacon.
(xiii)   The Boleyn Gate.
(xiv)   Church of St Mary, Culford.

Sir Roger de Trumpington

TRUMPINGTON

A Cambridgeshire Village

by EDITH CARR

Edith Carr (née Vincent) was born at Seven Kings near Ilford. She worked for a while in a lawyer's office in London, and it was during this period that she met the solicitor whom she married later. At the outbreak of the Second World War she moved to Cambridge with the Official Solicitor's Office that had been evacuated to Caius College. Since 1966 the Carrs have lived at Trumpington, a village with which her husband's family have been long associated.

The Manors

TRUMPINGTON had little recorded history until William of Normandy erupted into England. Its origin, however, can probably be traced to its position — a place where some of the ancient pre-Roman trackways met. The eastern track came over the Gog Magog hills to join with one coming from Essex and another from the north west. Where major tracks and people converged, small settlements began to develop.

Indeed, traces of this earlier civilisation in Trumpington were found at the beginning of the present century. On the east side of the Shelford Road, and opposite the main London Road, Iron Age pottery was discovered. Close by in Anstey Hall grounds remains of a Roman occupation were found, and the church and Anstey Hall are probably on the site of an early settlement. There are evidences, too, of another Iron Age settlement over the river at Grantchester. These two early inhabited sites lie on either side of what was doubtless an ancient ford across the Cam.

The Romans used this ford and left some of their pottery in the fields behind what is now Latham Road and Chaucer Road. It is probable that a Roman road ran from Trumpington to Cambridge through what today are fields to the farm at the river end of Latham Road; and from there along the edge of Coe Fen through to the bridge at Magdalen Street. Discoveries of Roman pottery and other remains on this line between Vicar's Brook and Trumpington Hall give greater emphasis to the probable existence of such a road. At some time the Romans discontinued their use of the Trumpington ford in favour of another three miles downstream, thus starting the early foundation of the City of Cambridge and leaving Trumpington to its agricultural growth, with its ford reduced to only local importance.

Later the Saxons established themselves here. This Nordic race mostly settled down in families, as their place names bear out, the syllable 'ing' showing kindred and 'ton' standing for town. An enclosure, perhaps fortified, within which all the family lived. So old Trumpington could have been the family settlement of a

Saxon chief with a name resembling Trumbeorht in its lengthened form.

Rural peace and quiet was at a premium in those days, as today, but for different reasons. There were always emergencies, some greater than others. If not the local marauder, it was the invader from overseas. Against the latter, to defend the country, not only the theyns, who anyway were bound by oath to fight, but the whole mass of the male population capable of wielding a weapon was called out. These levies from the shires formed the fyrd of England, a body of men not trained to war but for whom war was an occasional necessity.

When Cambridge was invaded by the Danes in 1010, men from Trumpington would have helped in the fight against the enemy.

In A.D. 991 Brithnod, Earl of Northumbria, set out to fight the Danes. He was refused hospitality by the Abbot of Ramsey, but at Ely he and his men were welcomed and feasted. Warmed by the wine and a generous spirit, he promised the Prior that Ely would receive many acres of land after his death. Brithnod fell in battle at Maldon and the monks of Ely brought back his headless body for burial in their priory church; recording among their new possessions four and a half hides of land in the village of Trumpington. This was about five hundred acres.

The land included the site of the mill later made famous by Chaucer, and probably also the ground on which the present church stands, and where the earlier church was. At the time nobody realised what a bone of contention this gift was to be in the following century.

As William made ready for his invasion he left nothing to chance. He wanted England and was going all out to get it. Not only did he gather his own barons, but he invited help from other countries. To adventurers the prospect was attractive. Battle under a renowned leader, with plunder and lands for the winning. No wonder Europe flocked to his standard. William de Warenne, Roger de Montgomeri, Count Baldwin of Guisnes, Alain de la Zouche, Eustace of Boulogne, Hugh de Montfort — names that were to pass into English history — joined with knights from Aquitaine and Poitou and adventurers from Piedmont and Burgundy. So that when the Doomsday survey came to be written with the names of England's new landowners set down for all time, those of the great barons appeared alongside minor knights previously unknown.

William's conquest of England was gradual and grants of land were handed out to the barons as each new area of land fell before the conquering armies. This meant that estates were widely divided, making any possible future rebellion difficult: no man would find it easy to collect his scattered forces with lords of nearby lands keeping a watchful and jealous eye on any proceedings. It also helps to explain the interchange of land between the various lords in later years, regrouping their possession to better advantage.

In 1085 William made his great land survey noting who held, what the land was worth, so that he might know what was due to him, and recording matters down to the minutest detail. The names of the new Lords of the Manors of Trumpington appear there, as well as those of the previous owners.

Put simply, a manor was an estate of land held of an overlord, either the king himself or a baron, with a condition of some form of service, usually military, attached to it. All land belonged to the king: but the barons could, and did, re-grant some of their estates, at the same time passing on the military responsibility to their tenants. So the lord living on his manor could have several overlords to whom he owed some form of service.

These are the names of the lords of Trumpington set out in Doomsday Book.

1066	Horulf, theyn of King Edward: Count Eustace of Boulogne
1086	Held by Ernulf de Aerda *(Possibly the Manor of Trumpington)*
1066	Tochi under the Church at Ely: William de Warenne
1086	Held by William de Cailli *(Cailli's Manor)*
1066	Horulf, the theyn: Picot de Grentebruge
1086	Held by Hervei *(Peverel's Manor)*
1066	Norman of Earl Tosti, a sochman of King Edward: Robert Fasiston
1086	Held by Robert, son of Robert Fasiston *(Possibly Arnold's Manor)*
1066	a sochman of Earl Wellef: Countess Judith
1086	Held by William de Evernay *(Possibly Beaufoe's Manor)*

The Picot who owned just over two hides of land in Trumpington was sheriff of Cambridge, King's collector of taxes in the shire. He was a hard man who extracted the utmost and expected more. Not only the landowners suffered under him: the local Saxons had to work on his farm, providing carts and lending plough teams nine times a year instead of three, as had been the custom in Edward the Confessor's time. They knew precisely what being conquered meant.

One of the great lords given land in Trumpington was William de Warenne. Four and a half hides, to be exact. Now this was the very piece of land that Brithnod of Northumbria had given to the convent at Ely, and by 1086 was held by William de Cailli under de Warenne. William of Normandy was a devout son of the Church — had not the Pope given his blessing to the proposed invasion? — but when Ely protested that the advowson was wrongfully held by the Caillis, its cries fell on deaf ears, for the Caillis held it until the fourteenth century.

A difficulty in tracing the lives of the early Lords of the Manors of Trumpington is that of deciding whether a William or a Simon is son, brother or cousin in the direct line. Men in the prime of life were claimed by war or pestilence, and often the heir was a minor in the guardianship of a relative, perhaps with the same name as his father: or it may have been a widow or a daughter. Under the law as it then stood, the barons had the right to sell in marriage, presumably to the highest bidder, the widows and daughters of their knightly tenants. Wealthy chattels of a deceased Lord of the Manor, they were sometimes pawns in an unscrupulous game played by a powerful baron overlord.

Their happiness was problematical: and the general result to the historian is often confusion.

In the year 1200 King John confirmed to William Valence, Earl of Pembroke, certain land in Trumpington, the Earl having made an exchange with the Count of Boulogne for land that he (Pembroke) held in Flanders.

Cailli's Manor

Of all the Trumpington manors handed out by William of Normandy to his followers the easiest to trace from the beginning is that of Cailli's, because the same family held it for two centuries.

In 1066 it was owned by William de Warenne. His family remained overlords, but the Caillis held it from 1086 (William); about 1164 (Ralph); about 1198 (Simon); about 1225 (John) for a minor in wardship (Simon); 1269 (Ralph); 1278 (Simon); and about 1303 (John).

John de Barenton married the widow of John de Cailli and in 1343 Bishop Simon de Montacute of Ely brought the advowson of the Church from them. This subsequently passed to the Prioress and nuns of Holywell Priory, Shoreditch near London, and after the Reformation to Trinity College, Cambridge, the present holders.

The manor itself passed by succession or purchase from de Barenton (or Barrington) to the families of Burgh, Ingoldisthorp, de la Pole, Neville, Scrope, Browne, Cutts, Chaplyn, Bacchus and Baron. The last named bought it in 1616. In 1775 one Crabtree, who had married the niece and heiress of the last of the Barons, sold to the Pemberton family in whose hands it still remains.

Trumpington Manor

The family of Trumpington's most famous parishioner, the Crusader Sir Roger, is not mentioned much till around 1200, but by that date seems to have been of some importance. Who was the first in the English line is not known. It could have been either the Ernulf or William of 1086, as both these names appear in the family tree. But descent of the manor can be traced from Roger's grandfather William, who died in 1218, to the acquisition by the present owners, whose family bought it in the seventeenth century.

"Land of William de Trumpington" is mentioned in 1204 and Everard de Trumpington was one of the sureties of Geoffrey de Lucy in 1207. At one time the Lucy coat of arms was to be seen in a window of the chancel.

Trumpington's Manor remained in the family until the fifteenth century and descends as follows: William (d. 1218); Everard (d. around 1259); Roger (d. 1289); Giles (d. about 1332); Roger (d. 1326); Roger (d. 1370); Roger (d. 1415); Walter.

Walter's sister Maud had married a John Enderby of Bedfordshire and in 1458 the heir to Trumpington Manor, Sir Walter's only daughter Eleanor, married her cousin Richard Enderby. This marriage produced a daughter, Alice, who inherited Trumpington's

Manor. She married one Pygot, of Shotton in Bedfordshire. In 1547 Francis and Thomas Pygot sold the manor to Edward Pychard of Trumpington, and in the sixteen hundreds the last of the Pychard family sold to the Pembertons.

While the family certainly held other land in the village in their own right, Sir Roger, as a free tenant, held from Simon de Cailli "a watermill and lands at 40 shillings yearly" and at his death in 1289 was recorded as having "a chief messuage (house) in Trompeton with a little vineyard, with lands and services held of the heirs of William de Ferrers; a watermill held of Simon de Cailli and land of John Bernard."

Roger's "little vineyard" would have been one of the many that flourished in England at this period. East Anglia was one of the three important wine producing centres in the country and indeed, the Isle of Ely was famous for its vineyards. But the weather was uncertain even in those days and this, coupled with the import of cheap Plantagenet wines from France, caused viticulture to dwindle in this country as a staple crop.

Peverel's Manor

Picot, Sheriff of Cambridge, was succeeded in his office by Pain Peverel, and the disposition of Peverel's Manor in Trumpington is interesting, because of its connections with families already mentioned.

The resident lord of the manor was Henry de Trumpington. From him it passed by descent to his son Walter; to Walter's son John: to John's son William and his wife Sarah, daughter of Simon de Cailli.

In 1547 this manor was sold by Francis and Thomas Pygot (who were our Crusader's descendants through the female line) to Edward Pychard of Trumpington, and was bought by the Pemberton family in the seventeenth century.

Arnold's Manor

Arnold's Manor got its name from John Arnold who held it under William Valence, Earl of Pembroke, in about 1290. Originally it had belonged to Count Eustace of Boulogne.

One of its tenants was Amy de Haukeston, who seemed to own the local gallows and a tumbrel. This latter was either a cart for ordinary farm use or a somewhat infamous stool used for subduing unruly females. For these essential items a yearly rent of seven pence was paid.

Through the female line Arnold's Manor came to a family named Charlton. Richard Charlton was either unfortunate or careless, because he was attainted by Act of Parliament in the reign of Henry VIII and his estates sequestered to the Crown — which granted the manor in Trumpington to a John Fortescue. He owned it till 1618 and was succeeded by Dr Eden, Master of Trinity Hall, Cambridge. On his death in 1645, Sir Francis Pemberton bought the estate.

There was only one other manor of any size, Byeufu (Beaufoes) or Crocheman. The holders of this are traced below.

Beaufoe's Manor

John (son of Walter de Trumpington) gave it to his son William and his wife Sarah, daughter of Simon de Cailli; knightly service for the manor was to be paid to Sir Ralf de Beaufoe. If William and Sarah had no heirs, the manor was to go to William's sister Christian; and if she died without issue, then to Sir Ralf de Beaufoe. (This is extracted from a deed of about 1280. The names of two of the witnesses at least are well known locally, Sir Richard de Frevile and Roger de Trumpington. . .)

Either death or a powerful baron overtook Christian, because we next find the manor in the hands of William de Beaufoe, having married Sarah, widow of William de Trumpington.

Their son Roger de Beaufoe sold to Sir William Crocheman, who died in 1332, leaving two co-heiresses, Mary and Elizabeth. Mary married John de Winceslow of London and Elizabeth, Ralph de Huntington. With the death of Agnes de Winceslow in the reign of Henry VI, the whole of the manor devolved on the Huntington family.

In 1443 Walter de Huntington gave the manor to his second son and in 1491 Thomas Huntington of Hempstead, in Essex, gave it to his daughter Margaret on her marriage to John Paris. It stayed in the Paris family of Linton, Cambridgeshire, for some years until Jane Paris married Thomas Cotton of Conington. About 1548 their daughter Eleanor married Edward Pychard of Trumpington.

From Pychard, by sale or marriage, the manor passed to Sir John Cutts and others, to Gardner, Handford, Bacchus, Thompson and, in the eighteenth century, to Christopher Anstey of Brinkley, on his marriage with Mary Thompson. From the Ansteys it passed to the Fosters who held it until about 1937 when on the death of George Cunliff Foster it was sold and became Government property.

Tincott's and Radegund's Manors.

In the words of William Cole, antiquarian and one-time vicar of Milton, Cambridgeshire, "There are other mushroom manors sprung up in this town, the one called Tincotts, the other Radegunds."

The first mention of Tincotts is in 1397 when Nicholas, heir to Sir John Francis, was said to hold one house, a dovecote, 2½ acres of land and a meadow called Bladwells. The tenant was Hugh Tincott.

Alas, this was another case of an unfortunate Lord of the Manor somewhere, because this small estate fell into the lap of one of the Barons of the Exchequer in about 1514. From there it passed into the hands of Elizabeth, Lady Scrope, and from her to George Dacre, ultimately being sold by Robert and Walter Dacre to Edward Pychard.

It seems Mr Pychard was acquiring quite an estate in Trumpington.

At some time during the reign of Henry II, Ralph de Cailli and William Fasiston gave land in Trumpington to the nuns of St Radegund's, Cambridge, so creating Radegund's Manor. This was absorbed by Jesus College when it was founded in 1496 by Bishop Alcock in place of St Radegund's. The nunnery was dissolved because "of the negligence and improvidence and dissolute disposition and incontinence of the religious women of the same house, by reason of the vicinity of Cambridge University."

This was something that Ralph and William could not have foreseen.

2   Justice

THE idea of government for the people and by the people is not new. It was there in the Saxon folk moots where "no man dictated: he might persuade, but he could not command". In mediaeval England the Shire Courts dispensed justice on these lines and so did the Hundreds under them, where village representatives sat in judgment on their fellows.

Trumpington, with eight nearby villages, made up the Hundred of Thriplow.

While it is true that redress for wrongs could be obtained at the courts, it must be admitted that probably their main purpose was fiscal — to put money in the royal coffers. And along with individuals, the Hundred itself could be fined for a crime or misdemeanour committed within its boundaries.

But justice could be tempered with mercy — from a higher court — because the records of 1188 note that "William de Warenne was pardoned 6/8 out of 100s. imposed on Thriplow Hundred for a murder". Ten years later some part of the Hundred belonging to the king himself was pardoned 4s. 2d. out of four marks imposed for a similar offence.

When the whole object of any fine was to put money in the royal coffers, it would not have been diplomatic to expect payment in full on a royal fine. But why was William granted relief? A pity the answer to this is not recorded.

One of the best defences any accused could put forward in a lay court was that he was a clerk. He may only have kept accounts for a merchant or penned the records for a lord of the manor, or been only just capable of reading a verse from one of the Psalms — known familiarly as "the neck verse". No matter, this gave him the right to call himself clerk and to plead benefit of clergy if accused of theft or murder, as quite a few of them were. This plea meant an immediate transfer to the Bishop's Court — out of the jurisdiction of the king's — and with the certain knowledge of a lighter punishment.

No wonder the laymen of the time viewed these courts with a jaundiced eye: their privileges were a growing source of irritation. They had no power of life and death, their punishments being limited to the ordering of penances. And however severe the penance, it scarcely compensated for murder.

Thomas Hardgare of Trumpington was before the Cambridge Assize Court in 1260 charged with the serious theft of stealing a lamb. He pleaded benefit of clergy and the Bishop's Officer removed him from the royal court. At the subsequent hearing before the bishop, Thomas was found not guilty and discharged.

But sometimes there were questions on a verdict. In 1339 Bishop Simon was required to answer why John de Herneys of Trumpington, when charged with theft, was set free by the Bishop.

This is his answer.

> John de Herneys was accused by John le Boter, before John le Fitzjohn Coroner of Cambridge, because he bought at Foxton in 1335 a Supertunic worth 2s. knowing that it was stolen at Kingston. Subsequently at Cambridge before John de Shardelowe in 1337 he asserted he was a clerk, was tried before us and acquitted.

The pace of justice could be very leisurely in those days.

The system whereby a man was equally responsible with his neighbours for their peaceable behaviour could have its drawbacks, especially when it came to paying a fine. Very ingenious were the arguments put forward to avoid this unwelcome sentence.

Again from the 1260 Assize Court records.

Stephen Greaves was bludgeoned and robbed on his way through Trumpington. As a result of his injuries Stephen died the next day. And because he died in Trumpington, the village was held responsible for his death. Yet at the subsequent Assize Court hearing the villagers successfully argued that the suspected man was nothing to do with them, but a stranger from another parish, with no assets to speak of.

A similar defence was put forward by the village spokesman when John Disce was accused of breaking out of the Trumpington mill of William de Bussey (where he had been put in custody) and killing a man in the process. But this time their luck was against them. The village was fined, not for the death of a man, but for allowing John to escape!

It might be argued that a man quick to use his knife — and there were many of them — deserved any punishment he got. But that accidental death could also draw a fine seems unreasonable.

Richard de Barent, intent on carting wheat in a Trumpington field, had the misfortune to fall from his cart. Poor Richard was killed outright. Now this meant a local enquiry to assess the value of the cause of death, in this case the horse and cart. For violent death meant payment of a deodand, that is a gift of money equivalent in value to whatever had caused the death. Theoretically, it was given to the Church for prayers for the unfortunate deceased, who had probably died unshriven. But practically, it was claimed by the sheriff.

The local jury probably knew Richard very well. Working in the same village he could have been no stranger to them, so charitably (for themselves and him) they under-valued the horse and cart at 9s. 3d. But somewhere suspicions were aroused, and the members of the jury found themselves up at the Assizes where they were collectively fined. Richard's accidental death became an expensive one for the village.

The story of the two boys in the field at Trumpington is incomplete and stark in its horror.

Of course they were strangers passing through, but they were tired, so they rested and slept in the mid-day break.

> And whilst one of them slept, the other arose and cut his throat with a knife and fled immediately. It is not known who he was, being a stranger. And the said injured one, by name Gerard as is believed, got up and went to the church of Trumpeton and barely lived for 14 days and then died . . . .

With no tears to mourn him.

Anyone wishing to escape the immediate consequences of a capital crime, meted out either by authority or with rough justice by friends of the victim, sought protection from the Church. Hotfoot they sped to clutch the sanctuary ring on the nearest church door. Once in the church they were safe from pursuit for forty days. Theoretically, that is, for usually the period of their stay was much shorter. The church itself was besieged. Armed men from the sheriff and friends of the victim kept a watchful vigil in the churchyard. No food supplies reached the criminal: there was no contact with the outside world. Without food and without hope, he soon gave himself up to justice.

This either meant allowing the law to take its course, or abjuring the realm. The choice was always the latter, though bleak its prospect. It was possible still to survive in a foreign land, while the chances of doing so in an English prison were slim. And so the criminal was given a port to make for and then took the abjuration oath.

> . . . . I do abjure the Land of our Lord King of England and I shall haste me towards the Port which thou hast given me, and that I shall not go out of the Highway, and if I do, I do will that I be taken as a Robber and Felon of our Lord the King, and that at the Port I will diligently seek for a passage and that I will tarry there but one Flood and Ebb, if I can have a passage, and unless I have it in such a space I will go every day into the sea up to my knees assaying to pass over; and unless I can do this within forty days I will put myself again into the Church as a Robber and a Felon of our Lord the King.

With all possessions forfeit he set off from the church gate, centre piece of a vivid little ceremony —

> ungirt, unshod, bareheaded, in his bare shirt as if he were to be hanged on the gallows, having received a cross in his hands.

John Miller of Trumpington killed his wife and then fled to Great Shelford Church for sanctuary. But events caught up with him there and he abjured, leaving behind his wordly goods worth a pathetic sixpence.

John Nichale took sanctuary in Trumpington Church confessing to many thefts. But the village would have none of him. A penniless stranger to the parish, he was doubtless forcibly helped on his abjuring way. Life for the mediaeval vagabond held more kicks than ha'pence.

Thomas, son of Trumpington's Walter the Plowright, was a hot-headed young man. He quarrelled, of all places, in the courtyard of Nicholas de Drayton, who was vicar of the parish. Thomas drew his knife (price 1d.) and stabbed John Wright of Girton in the stomach. And John died. Sobered by what he had done, Thomas fled to the parish church: some little time later he departed on his journey overseas, repenting his crime and all he was leaving behind. For he had been thrifty. He was the owner of "5 bushels meslin worth 20d; one quarter of barley 16d; 2 belts and one hatchet 2s; 1 adze 2 wymbles and 1 saw 6d; and one old tunic with cape 6d.

Walter must have missed him.

3   Mediaeval Times

S OME events of history are of such importance that they cannot be overlooked or forgotten. Such is Magna Carta. And probably the only good thing John did for his country was to die a year after signing it. For he had no intention of observing the terms of the Charter, and his sudden death brought to an end the civil war that had raged through England since that day at Runnymede.

The Trumpingtons were King's men, but John must have been too much, even for them. "William de Trumpington and those he leads with him have letters of safe conduct to parly with the King". So we read in 1216.

The following year William, Everard and Henry de Trumpington returned to allegiance. Bound by an oath of knightly service to the Earl, their overlord, they rallied to the cause of the child king, Henry III, under Pembroke's leadership. They could have been with him when he defeated the French in street fighting through the city of Lincoln.

William and Everard were notable men. William was a justice in eyre — what today we should call a judge on circuit — and Everard was a special justice, serving various offices under the Crown.

The Church played an important part in the lives and times of mediaeval England. Religious houses held vast tracts of land — frequently given with no more charge laid on them than that of the saying of prayers or the giving of alms. Even as early as A.D. 991 the convent at Ely became the richer, by 500 acres of Trumpington land.

Whether the de Caillis were pursued by guilt because the advowson of the rectory fell into their hands after the Conquest, instead of remaining in those of Ely, is questionable, but certainly this family gave generously to the Church.

The monastery at Bissemede owned thirty-five acres in Trumpington, given by Sir John de Cailli on no more return than the giving of alms to the needy: the Prioress of St Radegund's Nunnery in Cambridge held thirty acres on similar terms, the gift of Ralph de Cailli. Indeed, Ralph might have been accused of making sure of his reward in Heaven, so freely did he give to and for the Church. Seven acres to the Prior of Shengay; fifty-one acres for a house and land to the Rector of Trumpington; John Bernard held one acre of Ralph "by service of finding a lamp for burning in the Church" and Geoffrey Clark seven acres on similar terms for three lamps.

When John de Barrington and his wife, the former widow of John de Cailli, sold the advowson of the Rectory to Bishop Simon in 1343, perhaps Ely was appeased. But in the same year the tithes of the Rectory and the advowson (the right of presentation to the living) came into possession of the nuns of Haliwell Priory, Shoreditch in London with this proviso —

> that as heretofore the Prioress and Convent have received nothing for their clothing, the Prioress should receive 20s. the sub-Prioress 10s. and every nun 6s. 8d. from the revenues of Trumpington Church, to be employed in purchasing them the garments of their Order.

So the villagers of Trumpington helped clothe the holy sisters and gave of their first fruits; until finally the sweeping changes of the Reformation put the patronage of the living into the clerkly hands of Trinity College.

Edward II was an ineffectual king. His defeat at Bannockburn by the Scots in 1314 was a bitter blow to military pride. So much so that two years later the lords and knights of the shires of Cambridge and Lincoln promised Parliament the service of a foot soldier from every rural parish, who would be maintained by the parish. The men themselves were later "translated" into a sum of money assessed on the villages. Another form of tax, in fact, aimed at providing arms, wages and expenses for the forces of the king.

In 1318 the king's financial resources were at a low ebb. Where could he legitimately get money? There were outstanding debts to be collected, feudal obligations, and there were the East Anglian village levies, raised on the authority of the 1316 Parliament. So off went his special clerk to inquire into the matter.

What arms would be required by a foot soldier was apparently left to the villagers to define. And no inspiration came to

Trumpington. For of its levy of 24s. they paid the whole to the collectors for wages and expenses, "but did nothing to provide armour".

Money was always useful: and arms could be won, or collected from a dead comrade.

With depressing monotony the coffers of the English Exchequer needed frequent replenishings. The Parliament of 1380 voted a Poll Tax to help their insolvency, and the cost to the humbler people was the equivalent of a month's wages. This was bad enough, but Parliament also decreed that two-thirds of the tax should be paid within two months of its becoming law. Collectors were corrupt; taxpayers, as always, unwilling to pay and nothing like the hoped for sum was realised. So commissioners were appointed to investigate. Trouble loomed ahead which flared out into the Peasants' Revolt of 1381.

Starting in London the Revolt spread and within three days Cambridgeshire was involved. An approximate six mile radius of Cambridge was apparently trouble-free, but elsewhere for three days there were riots and trouble, to be followed by the days of reckoning.

Trumpington took no active part in the revolt, but Sir Edmund de la Pole, Lord of Cailli's Manor, was one of the special justices appointed to deal with the rebels.

Religious houses flourished in mediaeval England, though each nunnery rarely held more than thirty nuns. There would, of course be servants and a priest or two; there would also be hunting dogs, monkeys and other pets, all to help the sisters pass their leisure time. For many of them had no votive call to the religious life. The outlook was strictly practical. There was a limit to the welcome for maiden aunts, and if a girl missed marriage, then she must be placed in a nunnery. Sure of a welcome with the dowry she brought with her, the child — for she was very often little more than that — was respectably settled for life as a bride of Christ.

Small wonder that some of them broke their vows and escaped to a more virile world. Like Margaret de Cailli, for instance. Archbishop Courteney made a visitation of his Lincoln diocese in 1389 during the course of which he discovered her, a professed nun of St Radegund's, living in sin and in a secular habit. Guilty of a heinous crime, Margaret was returned to the Prioress of St Radegund's with instructions that she be kept in close confinement. Poor Margaret.

But a man could make a mistake in his vocation as well. John Mynetmoor of Trumpington was a canon of Anglesey Abbey. This notwithstanding, he absconded from there. There is no record of where he went, but he was discovered and brought before the Bishop at Ely charged with apostasy.

Some of the entries that come by way of the registers of the Bishops of Ely are quite exciting. Like these, for instance:

17 May 1346   Bishop's mandate for reconciliation of cemetery at Trumpington which has been polluted by bloodshed; the mandate to enquire when and by whom the latter was polluted.

While the Bishop was made aware of the facts, present day Trumpington is not, because no record was made, the next entry reading —

24 May   Trumpington cemetery reconciled, and later —

3 June   Order from the Bishop for dealing with the fees for reconciling the said cemetery which have been moderated from £5 to 5½ marks (around £2), because of the heavy expenses of the parishioners in the matter.

If only there were a little more information!

Bishop Arundel made an order in 1377 to the effect "that in view of the probable invasion of England by the French, clerics equally with laity may arm themselves." This was during a period when the fortunes of the Hundred Years War were against England.

Along with other landowners in the fourteenth century, the Church was responsible for helping to maintain the good condition of the highways, the actual work being carried out by tenants. This was fine in theory, but did not always work out in practice. So entries like this were frequent in the registers of other bishops as well as in that of Bishop Fordham. It reads —

Oct. 1390   40 days indulgence to all who within the next two years contribute to the repair of the Hauxton bridge and road.

Remission of punishment for sins, by a down payment of money for a useful cause, would often produce results where other methods failed.

Some of the inquisitions for tax purposes yielded surprising information. In 1399 there was an enquiry by Ely into the number of 'aliens' in the diocese. They were checking on the amount of monies going out of the diocese to owners other than themselves. One of these was the Prior of Lewes in Sussex, who was somehow entitled to a share of the parish tithes. His rather acid reply was to the effect that "from Trumpington he had received nothing these 25 years". Our forbears showing a good example of the Englishman's characteristic dislike and avoidance, if possible, of any form of tax paying!

In the same century Ely sent out a demand for the arrears of tithe owed by several villages. Trumpington's share was ten shillings and nine years later the debt was still owing. Who knows, it may be outstanding still.

It was not only the Church dues our village ancestors ignored. In 1500 Cambridge Town Treasurers "paid several labourers of Trumpington 13s. 4d. for cleaning a certain brook lying between Cambridge and Trumpington". After a lapse of two years there is another entry — "for the non-repair of Trumpington Ford, the liability to repair which was jointly shared by the inhabitants of Trumpington and the town of Cambridge, the inhabitants of Trumpington were fined 6s. and the town treasurers 3s. 4d."

This masterly inactivity on both sides must have produced an indescribable state in the ditch.

The parish church was the focal point around which village life centred. From birth to death it touched the lives of all. No records exist of the earlier church in Trumpington, but the present one is a fine example of fourteenth century architecture. The historian Blomefield says of it, "It is dedicated to St Nicholas and had a Gild of St Mary in it. Rectors presented vicars and in 1389 the nuns of Haliwell presented rectors".

A Gild of St Mary. No craft guild this, but rather a group of people — usually men — combining together for charitable or useful purposes. Perhaps this would be maintenance of a chantry or of a bridge, or the staging of a miracle play, often performed in the church itself.

There was also a Gild of the Holy Rood. For in 1521 the will of Richard Lambe of Trumpington was proved and among his bequests was one

> to the aldermen and brothermen twenty quarters of barley, for the best use of the Gild and repair of the Church.

All over the country there were many of these 'fellowship' guilds — with a strong religious foundation. They were in fact the forerunners of today's benefit clubs, and doled out help to sick and needy members. The guildhall itself was a centre of local life. Here the village met at supper on feast days; here they paid their offerings wrung from the soil; and here, on feast days and funerals, the members met and then went in procession to the Church. And when a brother could no longer work, the Guild funds made him a weekly allowance. Rich guilds had their own chaplain, living in the room above the hall and ready to help with difficulties in reading and writing.

In the Church is the base of the old village cross. This was dug up in 1921 from the site when the War Memorial was being erected and is the actual block of stone in which the shaft of the mediaeval cross was fixed. Like other crosses, including the one in the old churchyard, this would have stood on one or more steps. Its Latin inscription round the base reads "Pray for the souls of John Stokton and Agnes his wife."

It's fairly safe to assume that it was dug out from what was its original site, a place known to generations as Cross Hill. The cross itself would have suffered under the Act which set out that all crosses in any open place should be taken away and defaced before 1st November 1643.

While it was not uncommon for a man to leave money for the setting up of a cross, it is rare to find the cross inscribed.

At the end of the fourteenth century there was a John Stokton who was a tenant of Roger de Trumpington: he lived on the north side of Church Lane, not far from where the inn called the *Unicorn* now stands, in a house called Reynolds.

That Trumpington did indeed have a village cross is certain. John Layer of Shepreth writes in the early sixteen hundreds of "an old house belonging to Mr Pitcher (Pychard) against ye crosse" and churchwarden accounts of 1691 set out ". . .And lastly wee doe order an Exact Coppy of these presents to be forthwith written out and affixed on the publick Crosse of this Town of Trumpington to the end that none may pretend ignorance". So it would appear that at least the shaft of the cross was still standing then.

The "old house against ye crosse" contained several coats of arms, one of them being those of the Francis family who were Lords of Tincott's Manor. Could this have been the old manor house where Hugh Tincott lived?

Precisely what part the Trumpington family played in the building of the church is not known. Whether the partly visible mediaeval coffin in the outer south wall of the chancel is that of the founder, and whether that benefactor was a Trumpington, is only a matter for conjecture. But the magnificent fourteenth century canopied tomb in the north chapel may be that of Sir Giles, and his son Roger as well. They died within a few years of each other.

At some time the brass of the Knight Crusader was fixed on the table tomb; and it has certainly been there for well over three hundred years.

Blomefield, referring to the coats of arms on the brass says,

> There are two shields of the same on the south side (of the tomb) in memory of some of the Trumpington family, but now usurped by another with this inscription "Hic jacet Guilelmus Pycer . . . . A.D. 1614".

The coat of arms on the shield was carried by Roger and his son Giles: that on part of the brass (the same with a label of 5 points) by Roger, son of Giles.

4   The Parish

WITH parishioners generally averse to paying out money, the churchwardens must have been heartily thankful to those who did give, even if usually on approaching death.

In 1500 Robert Gardener left his body to be buried in the churchyard and five marks to buy lands for the repair of the church; three years later J. White left 40s. for the purchase of a Missal, and all his lands on the death of his wife. In 1671 William Austin, a tailor of Trumpington, gave fourteen acres of land in Bottisham and 20s. for coal for the poor. He had evidently suffered from the bad state of one of the local paths, for he left 20s. for its repair determined, apparently, that it should be well done. Ten years later Thomas Allen gave nine acres of land for the benefit of apprenticing poor children. He also added the treble to the ring of bells and gave the pulpit, which was originally in Emmanuel College.

It frequently happened, with so many livings being gifts in lay hands, that they were presented to people not in priests' orders at all. Peter de Rinallis may have taken holy orders, but he was certainly at one time treasurer of Poitiers in France. This should have helped with the ordering of Trumpington's finances when he became rector there in 1226.

But the parish priest on the spot was seldom the rector or vicar, but an underpaid chaplain or clerk, often as ignorant of the Latin words he mumbled as were his congregation. In a book published in 1559 on the life of Bishop Aylmer of London there is the apocryphal story of a vicar of Trumpington which bears this out. As related by Cole this appears —

> . . . . the comical story about the vicar of Trumpington who, reading ye Passion of Palm Sunday, when he came to ye exclamation of our Saviour, Eli, Eli, Lama Sabathari, stop short and calling to the churchwardens said, 'Neighbours, this gear must be amended. Here is Eli twice in the Book. I assure you, if my lord of Ely comes this way, he will have the Book. Therefore, by mine advice, we shall scrape it out

and put our town's name viz. Trumpington, Trumpington, Lama Sabathari.

Although the practice was frowned on, there was a great selling of benefices. With monotonous regularity during the sixteenth century the vicars changed at yearly intervals, and most of them probably never even saw their cure. John Skelton may have been one of these, for he seemed to be busy in other directions. Already Poet Laureate at Oxford, he received a like honour at Cambridge, being frequently employed by the University to write elegant letters on its behalf. In 1499 the University accounts showed two sums of 18 and 20 pence as "paid to the vicar of Trumpington for letters written by him to the King's mother" (Margaret Beaufort).

From Elizabethan times to the Commonwealth period, fees for christenings and burials were sources of income to the churches, especially those known as "pit money". These were for actual burials in the church itself, a legal right of every parishioner. These graves, known as lairstalls, were very popular — and highly toxic. The uncoffined bodies, placed in shallow earthen graves, were covered by a lairstone (sometimes with the addition of a brass inscription). These were frequently disturbed to admit of new interments.

Small wonder there were recurring outbreaks of epidemics!

One such burial must have been that of Agnes Perneys. Alas, only the record remains; the rest disappeared in the seventeenth century.

> Nere the Trumpington tomb in the Ile upon a ston in brass on the pavement — Of your charitie pray for the soule of Agnes Perneys, daur of John Perneys gent, wch died the 1st day of October in the years of our Lord 1559 on whose soule Jesu have mercy.

William Cole had a very perceptive eye. He lost no opportunity, either, for recording local history. At the funeral of his friend Mr Thompson he was able to note —

> The Altar is on two steps and very elegantly railed in. For about 8 feet wide before the Altar from it to the Rails is paved with black and white marble. Under the Altar and about 4 or 5 feet under the east wall in the churchyard is the vault of the Thompsons.

And when the vault was opened to admit of the remains of yet another Thompson, he saw there were about eight coffins already there and adds "I got my man to make a note of the inscriptions."

Presumably the service was just not quite long enough, because only four inscriptions were recorded, those of the later burials. So we shall never know whether that James Thompson who defied William Dowsing during the Commonwealth died of a peaceful old age or not.

> On ye plate of a coffin are blazoned: party per fess argent and sable crenelle, 3 hawks countercharged. Porter Thompson died ye 14 December 1754 aged 32 years.

> On another coffin plate is this: Miss Harriet Thorne died ye 7 December 1742 aged 2 years 5 months.

> On another with ye arms of Thorne impaling Thompson: under them is this inscription, Mrs Mary Thorne died 3 March 1742 aged 32 years. (Mrs Thorne was sister to the Mr Thompson)

> On another under the arms of Thompson is this wrote: James Thompson died 28 May 1743 aged 30 years.

In the chancel today are two illegible stones. But we know what they were once inscribed from Cole's notes. There is also a permanent record of the then vicar's asthma because, as he chattily says,

> Being here on Christmas Day when I officiated for my friend, Dr Barnwell, at that time very ill with an Asthma and Fever, I could read the epitaph; but could not make out about six Latin verses below.

The inscription was to an Edward Browning who died in December 1647 and the parish register of 1648 recorded on the 3rd of January following,

> Buried Mr Edward Browning Captain of ye Trained Band.

On the other stone was inscribed —

> Here lyeth the body of Mrs Katherine Baron, departed this life 20th day of October 1649 aged 45.
> > She that entombed Virtue in her Breast
> > Doth here entombed take her Rest.
> > Could Virtue Piety or Religion tied

Death's cruel Hands she had never died:
But shunn Death's cruel Darts none can for Why?
It is a decree of Heaven that all must die.

A sobering local example of a Cromwellian epitaph.

It is worth a mention that Trumpington Parish Registers are recorded as going back to 1671. Yet Cole makes reference to those of 1563. If he saw these around 1745 what happened to them? They could, of course, have been "borrowed" for reference. What a pity they were not returned.

The repose of one's soul meant a lot to the people of mediaeval England. And to ensure that it lay as peacefully as possible, those who could left property to the church, stipulating that the rents from it should be used for 'obits', when both the priest and the poor benefited. Obits were either in perpetuity or for a number of years.

It was an impressive little ceremony. On the eve of the anniversary the bellman went round the village calling out the name of the deceased and asking all who heard to pray for his soul. The grave was shrouded with a funeral pall and set out with wax candles. The sound of the passing bell was heard from earliest dawn and relatives and friends attended a requiem mass. Nothing was forgotten. Money to the vicar, to the parish clerk, to children and others who sang at the service, to the sexton, to the Gild and, most important, for bread and ale at the subsequent feasting. To the poor it must have been like going to a party, and awaited with just as much anticipation.

Then at one sweep all the lands devoted to "superstitious practices" fell into the hands of Henry VIII. And all the little lamps and candles were extinguished with the rents.

Officials from the Exchequer were sent to list the obit lands. In William Gaseley's account for Cambridgeshire he recorded for Trumpington,

> 3s. 1½d. of Richard Saye for free rent left for an obit
> 4s. 1½d. of Margaret Lakiners for house and 3 acres left for an obit.

There were probably more because, not unnaturally, many of the lands were "concealed" from the Commissioners. No less than twelve more searching visits were paid in the reign of Elizabeth, so the clearing up process was far from short.

Not only the lands. The Gild halls with their contents of furniture, brass pots and trenchers; their stock cows, corn and money — and their lamp and rood lands — were to be taken by the Crown. Henry's daughter, Elizabeth, carried on the work started by her father. One of the Patent Rolls of her reign records in 1569 that among forfeited lands sold by the Queen to William James Gentleman of the City of London and John Grey Gentleman of Nettlestead, Suffolk, was,

> Four acres of land in Trumpington called Touneland belonging to the chapel of Himtham and in the occupation of John Carewe and that tenement called Gildhall in Trumpington in the occupation of Thomas Pychard.

The People

5

THE names of those early owners of Trumpington roll out like cries across some old battle field — Cailli — de Warenne — Arnolde — Beaufoes — Quincey — de Montgomeri — Arundel — Valence — Mortimer — Trumpington — but really very little is definitely known about them. Dim shadows moving over a distant screen, sometimes only their coats of arms are left to remind us they were once connected with the village and surrounding lands.

But there are occasional glimpses of the Trumpington family. Sir Walter and his wife, Dame Anne, were buried in the Priory Church at Babewell near Bury St Edmunds. Edward II granted Giles de Trumpington the right to hold a fair, which was perpetuated until this century in the yearly village feast. Another Roger fought for the king at Boroughbridge in 1322 and the golden trumpets of yet another Trumpington were facing the gates of besieged Rouen in 1418.

They were a wealthy and powerful family. Even in the Crusader's time, they owned land outside Trumpington, for Sir Roger was also lord of the manor of Moggerhanger in Bedford. And the Trumpington lord who died in the mid-fourteen hundreds, owned as well the Cambridge manors of Newnham, Girton and Barton, and two others in Shropshire and Leicester.

Old records extol the virtues of the Crusader's grandson and his son, "They were both noble knights and brave soldiers". With so much apparent virtue in the family, its almost a relief to find that there was at least one recorded black sheep, aptly named, some might think, Nicholas. He met an untimely death, along with Sir John Arundel, when he was drowned "after having violated a nunnery near Portsmouth" in 1379. Some people might say this was a case of just deserts.

We know that William and Everard were king's justices: there were others who were lawyers, like Ralph and John. But besides eminent men of the law, the family also produced good fighting men. Everard's son, Roger, achieved distinction by accompanying the future Edward I to Palestine on the last Crusade in 1270, when the Prince captured Nazareth and almost died in the process of a wound from a poisoned dagger. And today the name of Roger de Trumpington is known in continents unknown in Roger's lifetime. For his vast funeral military brass is the second oldest church brass in England.

It must have been quite an undertaking, that journey from the village of Trumpington to that of Nazareth, and one not to be undertaken lightly. There was much to be arranged and considered. Who was to say that trouble would not arise at home? Some years of King Henry the Third's reign had been anything but quiet, with civil war tearing the country apart, peaceful though it was in 1270. A man must look after his own. So Roger made his arrangements and was given royal protection, over a period of four years, for all his lands and possessions.

But within two years the prince became Edward I, while to the coat of arms of the Trumpingtons was added the crosses of a knight crusader.

Roger had cause to be glad of Henry's royal protection. At some time he had become guardian of the heir and lands of the deceased Robert de Hardredeshull. Now the late Robert left an outstanding debt, money which had been "borrowed from the Jews" and by an ingenious arrangement this debt became repayable to the Crown. A demand had been made on Roger for repayment, probably even before he returned from Palestine.

The relief of the family can be imagined when the sheriff of Warwick was ordered "to respite until the quinzaine of Easter next the demand upon Roger de Trumpington for £252 and to restore his goods taken for this reason." £252 was a vast sum in the year 1273.

Six years after the accession of Edward he called thirty-eight knights to take part in a tournament at Windsor. One of them was Sir Roger de Trumpington. King Edward himself provided the knights' tourney apparel, and the bill for this is now in the Public Record Office. It makes interesting reading.

	s.	d.		s.	d.
Tunic	8	4	Leather quiret (throat		
2 ells of linen		8	protector)	3	0
Making and decorating			Straps		½
sleeves	1	8	Wooden Shield		5
Leather Helmet	1	4	Silvering same		8
" and parchment			Leather Ailettes		
crest		3	(shoulder pieces)		8
Sword of bone and			Embellishing generally		
parchment		7	with armorial bear-		
Silvering the blade		8	rings	19	0
Gilding the pommel		1			

With various other items for the horse, and including the cost of a journey from London to Windsor (which could be done for 2d. in those days) the cost was about £2. 4s. 7d.

And the scene must have been quite superb.

People of consequence were the Trumpingtons who kept the esteem of royalty through various reigns.

In the Court Rolls of 1378 is a reference to the Crusader's great grandson —

. . . . in the absence of Roger de Trumpington Knight, who is at sea on the king's service in company of John King of Castille and Leon and Duke of Lancaster.

Honours were heaped on them.

Henry IV died in 1415, but in February of that year by Letters Patent, 100 marks (around £200) per annum —with payment of arrears— was granted to Roger de Trumpington for life. Roger had scarcely started to enjoy this when the king died. But his son was no less generous. On the 16th October in the same year Roger surrendered this income, because Henry V bestowed on him "the keeping of the Priory of St Michael's Mount in Cornwalle in the king's hands on account of the war with France".

And in the following year two estates in Westmoreland "were granted to the King's knight, Roger de Trumpington" because their owner had been foolish enough to forfeit them through committing two murders.

Like his namesake forbears, this Roger was a soldier. He died in 1415, the year of the siege of Harfleur and the battle of Agincourt. One or other of these probably claimed him.

Old deeds in the possession of Jesus College tell more of those early inhabitants of Trumpington. Either late twelfth or early thirteenth century, these deeds throw some light on transactions between the Priory Church of St Radegund's and the various manor lords.

There is the contract between Reginald de Trumpington and the Prioress and her nuns. Margaret, his sister, was to become a novice with them, an arrangement whereby the nuns would benefit by "a rent of two shillings" due to Reginald from Thomas of Trumpington for "nine acres of land which Thomas holds of him: Thomas to render the services due to the king for the said nine acres."

When rents were as low as twopence, two shillings was a not inconsiderable sum. And with no fewer than sixteen witnesses, including William de Trumpington and his son Everard, to Margaret's taking the veil of a novice, her ultimate earthly destiny would have seemed in no doubt.

Then there was the Crusader himself, "for his soul and the souls of his ancestors" giving right of entry to the nuns into four acres of land in the Trumpington Field, with a rent of two pounds of cumin, an expensive crop, highly prized for its culinary virtues. Indeed, in another instance, Roger was the recipient of a rent of one pound of cumin, payable at Michaelmas, while Alice Sukling received "a rose at Midsummer". Much more romantic than a peppercorn rent.

The de Cailli family, too, find a place. For Simon de Cayli gave to the Church of St Mary and St Radegund one acre of land "for his soul and the soul of his wife Matilda who is buried there". For seven hundred years the bones of Matilda de Cayli have rested somewhere under the stones of Jesus College Chapel. Did those of Simon ever join her there, I wonder?

The powers of the old ecclesiastical courts were wide ranging and comprehensive. They covered all provinces of the Church, from the archdeacon's court to those of the bishops and archbishops. Every will of personal property had to be proved in either the bishop's or archbishop's court. And the registers of the Consistory Court at Ely faithfully set out particulars of the wills and intestacies of Cambridge inhabitants, and those of the surrounding areas, from the fifteenth century up to 1857.

From the Trumpington entries picking at random, there was Agnes Skeppe and the Greathead family; Oswald Kinge's intestacy in 1565 and the wills of Robert Ashby and William Atkyn. Peter Bett's will was proved in 1588. He was a man of property, owning land in Fenditton and Stowe as well as in Trumpington. There was no need for worry over his childrens' future. John and Ellen were well provided for.

And then again back to the Pychards — to 1576 and the will of Thomas Pychard, Gentleman. His manor of Trumpington and other property went to Frances his wife for life and then to his son, one boy among four sisters. Thomas was well blessed with this world's goods, as witness this gift "to my sonne William".

> I give to my sonne William my best silver sault doble gilt, six of my best silver spoones and my best silver pot doble gilt.

Men of substance indeed.

6   From Elizabeth to James II

WITH the wind of Reformation changes sweeping through the country, the clergy and churchwardens of the Cambridge deaneries met in Holy Trinity Church in early December 1550. And there an Order was read to them requiring "that all altars, whether of stone or other material, be wholly destroyed before Christmas Day next and congruous and decent tables devoutly and solemnly erected in their stead".

What Trumpington thought about this is not known. It complied with the requirement to destroy the altar, but where it put the "congruous and decent table", it certainly did not put it on the actual site of the old altar. For eleven years later Ely comments sharply on the parish —

> Parents do not send their sons or families to hear or be heard upon the articles of faith and other things required. No register of baptisms and burials kept, neither is there a book of homilies. The place where the altar stood not yet covered with stones and levelled.

In the same year Bishop Cox writes to Archbishop Parker about the living at Trumpington. Apparently the deacon for the parish, a certain Robert Hayles, had applied for this living and the Archbishop wanted a little more information. Poor Mr Hayles, he was certainly not to the Bishop's liking.

> He is not much evident in the parish but dwells at Trinity Hall, Cambridge. He is a B.A. He is not skilful at, nor specially licensed for preaching.

And, most damning of all, apparently, in the Bishop's eyes,

> He does not maintain hospitality.

After all that, it's not surprising that the living did not come his way!

Not all the Reformation changes were taken at a stride. Many of Elizabeth's subjects shared her pre-Reformation viewpoint that, having attended church once on the Sabbath, the rest of the day

(i)   The old Mill at the junction of Long Road and Trumpington Road about 1906.

(ii) Trumpington Church as it appeared in 1842.

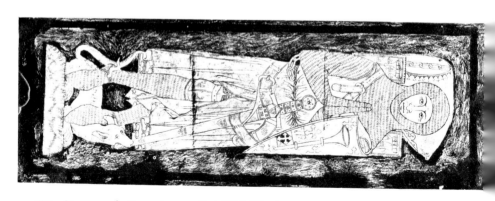

(iii) Sir Roger de Trumpington, died 1289. This brass is on a tomb in the North Chapel.

(iv)   Shepherd and sheep in a meadow near the river in the 1870s.

(v)   Part of the A10 Cambridge to Royston road at the beginning of the twentieth century.

(vi)   The blacksmith's forge in about 1880.

(vii)   The same blacksmith's forge in 1945.

(viii)   Trumpington men of the 'eighties. They were members of the Old School Club and the Tally Ho! Club. This photograph was taken on the occasion of a church parade and members of the Trumpington Brass Band are included in the group.

(ix)   The *Tally Ho* inn and the old Post Office opposite in about 1905.

(x)　The High Street looking towards Cambridge in 1923.

(xi)　The old *Red Lion* photographed probably in the 1920s.

(xii)　Almost certainly the original Whitlock's Almshouses.

(xiii)　Trumpington Hall, a substantially Georgian building with Tudor origins.

(xiv)   Wash day in Trumpington in the 1900s.

(xv)   The War Memorial on Cross Hill and the road to Granchester in 1921.

was theirs to do with as they liked. And so the Queen's subjects indulged in Sunday buying and selling; they wrestled, fought and played, often in the churchyard itself. For this and other misdemeanours they could be brought before the Courts, if unlucky enough to be caught. Like John Chapplyn, for instance. He was prosecuted in the Church Court for "brawling in the Churchyard". John, and many others, obviously paid scant attention to the sober viewpoint that Sunday should be spent in prayer and meditation. Indeed, to remind people of their duties, the homily of "the Place and Time of Prayer" was appointed to be read in all churches in 1574. It came down severely on

> the wicked boldness of those that will be counted God's people, who pass nothing at all of keeping and hallowing the Sunday. . . . they must ride and journey on the Sunday; they must drive and carry on the Sunday; they must keep markets and fairs on the Sunday; they must row and ferry on the Sunday. . . . they will not rest in holiness as God commandeth; but they rest in ungodliness and filthiness, prancing in their pride, pointing and painting themselves to be gorgeous and gay; they rest in gluttony and drunkeness like rats and swine; they rest in brawling and railing, in quarrelling and fighting, they rest in wantonness, in toyish talking, in filthy fleshiness; so that it doth too evidently appear that God is more dishonoured and the devil better served on the Sunday than upon all the days in the week beside.

Seeds of the Puritan epoch were germinating. But even so, authority had no easy task in seeing that the letter of the law was obeyed.

An early Chaplyn fought in the churchyard, but a later member of the family was one of the Lords of the Manor. Not only that, he had a hand in helping to supply the town of Cambridge with water. For in 1630 Thomas Chaplyn, then Lord of the Manor of Trumpington de la Pole agreed to the diversion of water from Nine Wells across the common field of the village and down to Trumpington Ford in connection with "the new channel or rivulet running between Cambridge and Nine Wells in Trumpington Fields and thence into the King's Ditch".

Thirty years later either this man, or a son named Thomas, was Member of Parliament for Bury St Edmunds. A far cry from the yeoman, John, who brawled in the churchyard.

After the Reformation, and particularly during the reign of Elizabeth, the powers of churchwardens greatly increased. In addition to their church duties, there were other responsibilities. They had to ensure there were arms for the trained bands, or militia, that roads and bridges were maintained, the stocks and whipping posts in good order and, with the assistance of the parish constables and overseers, helped to round up vagrants and succour the poor. More of a burden than an honour, it was not a popular office; the turn on the rota was awaited with a gloom of anticipation and the reins of office were joyfully relinquished.

Then there were the Bishop's visitations when an account was required of the churchwardens. And not only of things related to the church, either, for the inquiry covered the lives of both the parson and his people. Did the priest wear the right vestments; did he catechise and instruct the youth of the parish; was the parsonage house and glebe kept in good order? Were any of the parishioners guilty of adultery, swearing, refusing to come to church, indulging in unlawful work or recreation on Sunday, or brawling in the churchyard? Never had Church and State so combined to play watchdog. The churchwardens pried and probed into village morals and general behaviour, from the priest in the parsonage to the cottager in the croft.

The presence of an illegitimate child would send the church-wardens in a vigorous search to discover the father, so that the offspring would not be a burden on the parish. This was no easy task, for often the mother refused to divulge the name and the father was adept in concealing his identity. It was natural that neither wished to appear before the justices. Sometimes they found willing helpers in keeping the birth a secret, though this was a penal offence, as was sheltering any such unfortunate girl. Even the marriage rite held no absolute safety, for to produce a child before nine months had passed could lead to trouble with the bishop.

Matthew Wren was Bishop of Ely from 1638 to 1667. Eighteen of these years he spent in prison during the Commonwealth. A High Anglican like his Archbishop William Laud, he zealously set about introducing reform into the churches in an area of England where the inhabitants are obstinately opposed to change. The questions in his Visitation of 1638 are formidable. The church-wardens must have been appalled at the task set them. Certainly they were aggrieved at having to pay for their answers being written in a clerkly hand. For when Wren was accused in 1641 one of the charges against him was that

> the Churchwardens and other men sworn at the Visitation were forced to have their presentments written by clerks, to whom they paid excessive sums of money for the same, some two and twenty shillings . . . . to the grievous oppression of his Majesty's poor subjects in that Diocese.

Wren churned up a sea of discontent in the parishes until it seethed and bubbled over in his impeachment.

Trumpington answered that its vicar was Francis Halfheide, who was also the schoolmaster, and the churchwardens were Edward Wilson and John Eusden. Our erring parishioners presented at the Consistory Court in this year were —

> Thomas Squire for refusing to come to the holy table to receive the communion;
>
> Janet wife of William Ames for coming to be churched without a vayle. Certified it was a mistake.
>
> Goodwife Goodwin for living from her husband. (A man living apart from his wife was subject to a fine of seven shillings. Was the goodwife fined the same?)
>
> Mr Thompson, farmer of the rectory, to unstop the chancell windows.

The restoration of Charles II saw Matthew Wren restored to his bishopric and within two years, 1662, he held his second visitation, when the state of Trumpington Church was graphically described by its churchwardens, Richard Baron and William Green.

> Our glass windows are broken as well in the chancel as in the body of the church . . . .
>
> We have no altar cloths, save only very coarse.
>
> We have not yet the sacrament off the altar set up, nor decent hangings above the altar, nor a table off the back side of the altar. No locks on the church gates. One window in the chancel wanteth iron bars and glass also. It is only as yet shut up with a board.

And true to the occupation forced upon them by virtue of their office — that of village snoopers — they reported that

> A certain woman named Johan Whitley hath a child which she said was John Peck's.

Matthew Wren was an industrious bishop. He spent more years in prison than he did in his bishop's palace, yet in that time he achieved much. He catalogued many of the documents and papers relating to the diocese, with brief outlines of their contents. In the succeeding Commonwealth years many of the original documents were lost or destroyed, so that Wren at least preserved for posterity the record of what had irretrievably gone. In the first year of his installation he held a visitation. Neither imprisonment nor age daunted him. Although he was seventy-four when restored to Ely, he managed two more visitations before his death at the age of eighty-one.

His last visitation, as thorough as ever, was held in 1665. Rowland Frances and William Emerson were then churchwardens in Trumpington and they had quite a little list of reparations.

> The church and steeple want plaistering without, the pidgeons to be kept out.
>
> Font to be taken up and searched and a new cover to be made.
>
> A chappell on the north side out of repairs in timber in leddes and lime work to be amended.
>
> The pulpit and desk to be hung with greene cloth fringed. The church and chancell to be new whited and plaistered and the chancel pavement mended.
>
> A carpet for the communion table (this was made of silk, entirely different from what we know today as 'carpets'), a napkin for the same and a new Patten for the Communion Cup, Jewell's works and a book of homilies, a book of homiiies to be provided.
>
> To certifie of 3 locks to the church.

Trumpington was not the only parish with font trouble. Out of sixty-nine churches reported on, fifty had defective fonts in that either the water would not stay in, or else it would not run out. Hence the "searching". And the order for the new paten was one shared with many other parishes, namely, that the existing one was to be made larger.

About 1280 a marriage between the Trumpington and Cailli families started the line of Beaufoes Manor. The ownership passed through various hands until, in the reign of Elizabeth I, it was bought by Edward Bacchus "who built a faire gentleman's house upon it and his son, Bartholomew Bacchus, was owner of it".

This family lordship was short-lived, because the third generation Bacchus sold to James Thompson. And James Thompson was quite a character. A J.P. and yeoman farmer rapidly becoming a gentleman of means, his motto might have been "I protest".

When the impeachment of William Laud, Archbishop of Canterbury, was imminent in 1640, Cambridgeshire was preparing its own petition to Parliament, charging Matthew Wren, their bishop, with fostering idolatry and superstition. This petition, now in the British Museum, was signed by gentry, clergy, yeomen and peasants alike. There were more than a thousand signatures. The petitioners blamed the Bishop, his Chancellor Dr Eden and others under them, for the injuries done to their consciences and estates. Perhaps the injuries done to the latter, through their pockets, governed the extent of their indignation.

The first signature is that of Thomas Pychard, Sheriff of Cambridge in 1639 and Lord of Trumpington's Manor. Under this is the neat writing of James Thompson, followed by the names of Edward Browning and Katherine Baron, all resident in Trumpington.

Having registered his early disapproval of his bishop, in 1643 James Thompson again protested, but this time for the Church. Cromwell's henchman, William Dowsing was on his fanatical tour of Cambridgeshire churches and only at Trumpington were his orders disobeyed, as Dowsing had to record.

> March 5 Trumpington. 3 superstitious Pictures, the Steps to be levelled, which Mr Thomson to whom we gave order to do it, refused.

The "superstitious pictures" would have been figures in stained glass and the two steps at the altar rail remained untouched until about 1851.

Three years later Mr Thompson was again protesting: and this time it was recorded in the House of Commons Journal. For James Thompson was injudicious, or brave, enough to comment that Sir John Evelyn had said "that it was time to send for the Army to curb the pride and . . . of the Mechanick Citizens". This resulted in his being sent for as a "Delinquent" by the Serjeant at Arms and his expulsion from the Commission of Justices of the Peace.

There were later Thompsons. Indeed, there were other Jameses. And how different was the James Thompson who died in 1743 —

at the age of thirty — from his great-grandfather! William Cole was a family friend and he says of him,

> He absolutely killed himself with drinking, not knowing how to spend his time after coming to ye estate, being quite the reverse of his brother, who was a man of excellent parts and reading.

The Barons were a very old Trumpington family. A John Baron was churchwarden in 1599; another Baron filled the office in 1662; and the family became Lords of Cailli's Manor (by purchase) in 1616.

William Cole etches a picture of the Baron of his time — rather poignant now in the knowledge that this was the last in line of the male Barons.

> Mr Baron, my father's old friend, lives in Trumpington where he has a good estate, fine groves and fishponds. But his chief pride is in his hedges and sheep, exceeded for beauty by no one. He is now very infirm and a cripple, yet never-the less is constantly on horseback, though he cannot get up or down without assistance.

The estate passed in line to a niece, who married a man named Crabtree.

Samuel Peck, vicar of Trumpington, joined William Cole for coffee one day in March 1776, and the vicar of Trumpington confided to the vicar of Milton "that he had purchased of Mr Crabtree, on February 13 last, the manor of Cailli's". Then William Cole adds another note to his copious records.

> Mr Peck's manor was last in the hands of the Pychards, the last of which name married his maid servant and was supposed to have been made away with and buried in the garden, where a skelton was found some years ago.

So runs rumour. And accuses the wife.

The actual burial place, however, is still a mystery. For while other Pychards are buried in the church, including his infant son of a few weeks, the remains of Thomas, erstwhile Sheriff of Cambridge, are not recorded there. But then the Commonwealth period was a very unsettled one in which to die.

The good vicar of Trumpington was a little inclined not to check up thoroughly on all his facts. Some of his information is inaccurate including that – probably much to his disappointment – about the purchase of Cailli's manor.

Thomas Pychard's widow married a James Whitlocke by whom she had two sons, James and George. In 1665 the name of James Whitlocke first appears, on the churchwardens' accounts. Thereafter for some years it occurs regularly. The names of those who gave to "ye relief of Shadwell and Wapping by fire" is headed by Sir James Whitlocke, who contributed one shilling. Lest this be thought a niggardly sum, it must also be recorded that the same amount came from Mr Thompson, Mr Baron and Mr Thomas Allen.

In the High Street at Trumpington stands a modern home for old people called Whitlocks. What stood there before was known for years as Whitlock's Yard and was probably originally the garden of a Whitlocke, perhaps even that of Sir James himself, most certainly George's.

George Whitlocke left his house and its appurtenances to the poor of Trumpington, with explicit directions as to the application of the rents. He may have died a gentleman, but one of the meaner sort. The coals for the poor were to be of the cheapest: the coats and caps, given annually to eighteen poor people, were constant reminders to all of his munificence, bearing, as they did, brass badges with the initials G.W.

Now in 1818 George Whitlocke's bequest consisted of an old house and garden, with the remains of a malting. And in this year a change took place. For the buildings were altered into nineteen cottages and the land divided into twenty two small gardens, all ready for letting.

A photograph, possibly taken in late Victorian times just before the buildings were demolished to make way for a nineteenth century development which became known as Whitlock's Yard, almost certainly shows Whitlocke's house and garden after the conversion. Of similar construction to another one in the village, its date is about 1654.

From time to time special collections for worthy causes are found in the parish records. Possibly the earliest of these is the four shillings subscribed in 1306, by way of Peter's Pence, for the upkeep of a college in Rome for English students.

In latter years a brief, or letter of request, was issued by the Crown, or a bishop, or even a local magistrate. This was for help in some calamity, quite often a fire. The letter was read out at morning service and the churchwardens stood at the doors as the people left, ready to accept their contributions. The Parish Registers record a sum of three shillings collected in 1679 "for Ampthill in Bedfordshire"; two years later 3s. 5½d. was collected "for ye relief of ye Protestant in Little Poland" and in 1693 Trumpington was moved to give 8s. "for ye French Protestants".

From 1681 until 1698 there are many entries of donations for losses by fire. East Dereham, Caistor, Southwark (where it must have been fun for the fire fighters as the fire was in "ye maze"), St Katherine by the Tower of London, Drury Lane, Stafford and "Churchill in Oxon".

Then there were other appeals. For example, the parish must have felt very strongly about "redemption of the King's subjects in captivity at Algiers". They responded magnificently to the tune of £1. 8s.

Judging by some of the entries, the sixteen eighties must have been calamitous, weather wise. In 1682 Trumpington gave 2s. 4d. "towards rebuilding of Eynesbury Steeple, Hunts". Six years later the "lossess by earthquake at Kettleworth, Yorks" merited 4s. 4½d. from the parish. It was unfortunate that the next disaster came only two months after the earthquake, because Trumpington could only afford 2s. 6d. for "loss by overflow of waters in Cumberland".

These three entries —

		s.	d.
Oct. 1691	Teignmouth Devon, pounded by ye French Navy	5	0
May 1692	Clopton, Norwich, suffered by casualties at sea	6	6
Sept. 1692	Duridge Witherington Northumberland, loss by French privateers firing and pillaging	2	5

are a reminder of a depressing period of our military history in the reign of William and Mary. The sun of Louis XIV of France was shining too brightly in English eyes.

The weather was not the only worry troubling England in 1688. The king made a contribution too. James II was a good soldier but a poor monarch, whose actions soon incurred him the enmity of his people.

In 1689 thirteen apprentice boys closed the city gates of Derry in Ireland against the invading forces of James II. This event is now celebrated ardently each year. Yet England must have felt sorry for their besieged fellow Protestants. Trumpington alone "for the relief of the Irish Protestants" sent £3. 16s. It may have been hatred of the king and his religion, and of his attempts to impress Roman Catholicism again on his people. If so, one small village strongly showed disapproval by the amount of money collected.

Village Life

HOUSES of wood and thatch largely predominated in the village, with a consequent high fire risk. There are records of several Trumpington fires where the barns, ricks and granaries were burnt out. These fires must have taken in small cottages in their flaming stride and destitute families had perforce to rely on charity.

All over the country the number of indigent poor had increased. There were more people — and fewer jobs in agriculture because large tracts of arable land were being turned over to pasture. And not all the unemployed remained honest. Some became part of "a rowsy ragged rabblement of rakehells", a preying terror on society.

To deal with the situation an Act of 1601 brought into existence Overseers of the Poor. A parish rate was levied, the main purposes of which were to give weekly financial relief to the sick, the old and the weak; to set up a workhouse for ablebodied vagabonds and provide materials for their work; to build houses for homeless and destitute families on common or disused land; and to see that orphans, waifs and children of the very poor were educated by being apprenticed.

In the early enforcement of this act 'vagabonds' received short shrift. They could include the wandering pedlar and minstrel, and even the travelling scholar who, without testimonial or licence and not being local, found themselves whipped, or placed in the stocks. Sent on from village to village with like treatment, they reached their home town aching, bruised and bloodied.

Trumpington whipping post, now in the Cambridge Folk Museum, would have held many such a one chained for correction.

The more humane treatment of later years produced such entries as this from Elias Bland, the Constable in 1771,

13 Apr.	Gave a man	2d.
15 "	Gave 5 poor men	6d.
" "	Gave a poor man	2d.

29 May	Gave 4 men	6d.
,, ,,	Gave a woman and 3 children	3d.
,, ,,	Gave 4 men	6d.

There must have been some sort of scale for poor relief: women and children were obviously in the lower levels!

It was 1790. Young Mr Pitt led the Government in London; George Washington became the first President of the United States; and William Ostler, Constable at Trumpington, recorded his account for the Parish Council, entering for May,

Gave a poor old soldger	4d.
Gave a soldger and 2 saylers	6d.
Gave 2 saylers and a weaver	9d.

Life went on.

Even in the Registers, there was proper regard for the hierarchy of the parish. Death was no leveller in the records and courtesy titles were given.

Buried Sir James Whitlock	1700
Buried George Whitlock Gent	1724
Buried Lady Whitlock (widow of Sir James)	1715
Buried Mrs Catherine Whitlock	1742

The missing old registers also apparently recorded the deaths of a Samuel Norman, Scholar of Christ's College, in May 1647 and of James Thompson in 1670.

But sometimes there was not even a name. Like this entry —

8 August   Poor Traveller's child buried.

Epitaph for the brief life of the babe of some wandering mother.

Benefactors of the Church and parish were remembered with a short biography.

1692   Mr Thomas Allen buried. He sojourned in his old age in this parish . . . . followed by a list of his gifts at length.

1679   William Austin, tailor
. . . .and a list of his not inconsiderable legacies. But benefactor though he was, there is no 'Mister' for William. *He* was in trade.

Now the Revd. John Barnwell was so anxious to record his mother-in-law's gift that it inadvertently found its way into the baptisms. Sandwiched between the names of two newly arrived parishioners is this entry —

> 22nd Apr. 1738   The green velvet cushion for the pulpit was given by the worthy Mrs Fountain.

Some gave land, others coal. But did Mrs Fountain, worthy though she was, ever dream that she would be remembered only for her green velvet cushion?

There is even a record of an excommunication. In the top corner of a flyleaf is this, "George Lamb, William Aunger, Lancelot Younghusband, Lancet Young; excommunicated for contumacy by Dr Cook and declared so to be by me, William Baylie 1677." Parson Baylie could have enlarged on these facts to our advantage.

William Stacey was a farmer. He rented Rectory Farm and lived in the Rectory house. He was also a churchwarden and his expense account of small outgoings throw a light on Trumpington village in 1732. The biggest is for 8s. 2d. for "bread and wine at ye sacrament". Compared with other items this seems excessive; but then all over the country large quantities of sacramental wine were consumed generally in the parishes. For some it was their only opportunity to drink wine and they took advantage of it. Naturally they drank deep.

These are William's other expenses:

		s.	d.
29 June	for going to Bishop of Ely's visitation	1	0
11 Oct	ye Ringers at ye King's coronation	5	0
5 Nov.	ye Ringers at Gunpower Treason	6	8
	paid ye Ringers at the King's proclamation	2	8
	Thos. Baron for 2 hedgehoggs		4
	to Edward Newman for making a path to ye church door	1	0
	for washing ye surplice and scouring ye plate	2	6
	Thomas Watts for 2 polecats		8

Evidently someone decided the ringers were making a good thing out of the special occasions when they rang a peal of bells for the parish. For in 1738 it was agreed "for the future to give to the ringers only on 5 November and the King's Coronation

Day". What the ringers thought about this can be imagined. The Stacey family were bell-ringers. One of them, Francis, carved his name and the date 1732 in the ringing loft. He was a member of the Society of Cambridge Youths (Bell ringers), in whose records he appears as "Francis Stacey, Farmer, Trumpington".

Several names run through the pattern of Trumpington's history like threads recurring in a tapestry. Few reached the twentieth century, but two which did are those of Haslop and Haggis. There was a Haslup christening in 1589 and in 1660, "Thomas Hazlip, sonne of John Haslip, was baptised".

In 1691 Avice, daughter of William and Martha Haggis, was baptised. Two years later a son was baptised. They called him Bransum. Over two centuries have passed but now, in 1970, the descendant of that Bransum still lives in Trumpington and bears his ancestor's name, though it is now spelt Bransom.

With no purchase or selective employment tax to be added wages and prices, like the standard of living, were not high. For half a day's work in destroying sparrows in 1790 somebody got paid sixpence and probably thought it well worth while. Beer was 3d. a quart, cleaning Church Lane cost 6d. and 5s. 3d. was paid for decreasing the mole population by 3¼ dozen.

If this was considered the rate for the job, it's not surprising that some families were hard put to it to make ends meet. So the parish granted them relief. In 1772 certain poor people were exempted from rates on account of "the dearness of the times".

Large quantities of "powder and shott" were used and sedge turves were dug out for burning. In 1778 new shoes for Ann Colles cost 3s. 10d. and a pair of leather stays for her 5s. 9d. Oak posts were 8d. a foot and Robert Coleman received 1s. 6d. for going with the children to be confirmed. And a carpenter's bill for work in the church reads —

		s.	d.
1776	For work and wood at the little bell	1	0
"	" " " " " grate bell whell	13	0
	A round to the latter		2
	For nails (and hand made at that)		8

However healthy an open air life can be, the housing conditions of the working classes were anything but, so that when epidemics broke out the sickness ran like wildfire from family to family. In

1783 there were seventeen ill of the smallpox in Trumpington. Three people died. Five years later one hundred and seventy-nine people were infected. But the parish had been inoculated and of these only one villager died and apparently his death could have been attributed to other causes. By 1808 inoculation was general, "Mr Okey inoculated 90 people, some of them at their own expense." Medicine was winning.

In the year that Napoleon invaded Egypt and lost his fleet to Nelson at the Nile, the British Government were seriously considering a possible invasion of England by the French. For in 1798 they issued an order. A general account was to be taken of all cattle and of people willing to help in case of invasion. And so that the situation should be thoroughly understood, the inhabitants of Trumpington were called together to listen to "An address on the probability of invasion".

> We are met to consider how we may best comply with the order of an Act of Parliament lately passed to enable His Majesty most effectively to provide for the defence and security of the kingdom and repel an invasion of it by His Majesty's enemies. It will be proper to inform you that there is nothing in this Act which compels any man to perform any service which he is not inclined to . . . .In order to know the real strength of the kingdom it is necessary to take an account of the number of men between 15 and 60 years of age and to make a return of those who are willing to engage themselves to be armed trained and exercised for the defence of the kingdom. The act expressly provides that you are in no case to be called out but upon the actual appearance of the enemy.

Then follows the duties of pioneers and volunteers, the first being "to remove the women and children to a place of safety". With the very real fear there was of Napoleon Bonaparte at that time, one wonders where that would have been.

Pay was to be eighteen pence a day, picks, spades, shovels, hooks and axes to be provided by recruits.

The address goes on—

> I believe there are few parishes in which a considerable number have not come forward to offer their services and I hope you will not be more backward than others or less willing than your neighbours to lend assistance in the time of danger, or to join

in repelling the attack of a mad and desperate enemy. . . .I should hope we have so much of the old English spirit left that there will be no one so mean or so base as not to do everything in his power to defeat their designs and save his country from the disgrace and misery of French power and French cruelty.

A very mistaken notion prevails among some of you that your condition would not be altered for the worse should the French succeed. . . . we must look and see what they have done in other countries. . . . the poor labourers of Germany could give you such horrid accounts of their tyranny and cruelty to them as would induce you to think that they would not be less merciful to Englishmen whom they hate and detest.

After this epic speech it's not surprising that the old English spirit surged right up in Trumpington and one hundred and twelve volunteers stepped forward.

What is interesting in today's eyes is the agricultural strength of the village then. There were seventeen waggons and five carts; eighty cows, two hundred and twenty pigs and fourteen hundred sheep; eighteen riding horses, forty colts and seventy draught horses.

There was strong religious prejudice in this country against any sort of a census of population. Look in the Bible and see what happened when David numbered the people. Pestilence was the reward for his vainglory. Let it not happen to us. But Parliament at last took a firm stand in 1801 and the ten yearly census became an established act. Not that at first people were any less suspicious, or that the returns were always accurate. For instance, in 1811 there were ninety-five families in Trumpington and twenty-four of these were Dissenters. This, according to one clerk, made a proper return of seventy-five families!

However, by 1831 the ten yearly census had become an accepted part of life, though the clerks probably grumbled as they laboriously marked off the numbers of families in single line digits.

To those of us who have coped with what seemed irrelevant questions on today's census forms, the Population Enquiry Formula One of 1831 looks refreshingly simple. Here are Trumpington's replies.

Inhabited Houses	136
Families	149
Houses building	2
” uninhabited	3
Families employed in —	
Agriculture	85
In trade and manufacture	30
All other families	34
Males	357
Females	365
Males upwards of 30 years	170
Agriculture —	
Occupiers 1st class	11
” 2nd ”	5
Labourers	80
Manufacturers	80
Retail trade and handcraft	32
Wholesale and Capitalists, Clergy, Office Clerks, Professional and other Educated Men	5
Labourers not agricultural	4
All other males of 20 years	28
Male Servants over 20	5
” ” under 20	3
All female servants	20

There were, alas, no canal diggers in this parish.

8   The Changing Times

THE agricultural revolution is well-known history. Enclosure of the great open fields into smaller units fenced with hedges, as we known them today, made for improved farming methods. Thousand of acres of waste and woodland added to the arable lands. Agriculture was booming. New crops and new methods of farming were introduced and larger strains of cattle grazed in the pasture lands.

Prior to this the peasant had his strip in the great open corn-field. Maybe it did come between those belonging to a larger landholder, but it was his, and his family's before him. He had a right to pasture his cow on the common, to let his pig loose on the wasteland, and to gather brushwood for fires. All this helped him to eke out a living which, however frugal, kept him a free man.

But someone has to suffer in the name of progress. In this case it was the small owners of land and peasants with their feudal rights in the soil. The small owner sold out his land and the peasant lost his independence.

The idea of enclosing open land was not new. It had been there in Tudor times. Indeed, in Cambridge itself then there were complaints, and even rioting, because it was felt that the town bailiffs were enriching the Corporation by enclosing common land. Unemployment caused by local enclosures was the cause of the revolt led by the Norfolk tanner, Robert Ket, in 1549.

But while in Tudor times the Government was half inclined to sympathise with the peasants who saw the enclosing as a public crime, by the eighteenth century it had moved into the opposite camp which regarded enclosure as a public duty.

The Vancouver Report of 1794 says of Trumpington,

> There is no enclosure at present in agitation, though the want of such an improvement is much lamented by the most thinking farmers, who are extremely desirous that at least the intermixed property should be laid together.

Wholesale private Acts of Parliaments were hurrying through the legislative chambers of George the Third's government between 1760 and 1820 to speed up the general work of enclosing. The resistance of small owners was ironed out: each had to be content with what was awarded him in compensation by the Parliamentary Commissioners. And how could a small man afford to enclose and drain a distant acre in the new shape of things? His only course was to sell out to the owner of one of the new compact farms which were rapidly replacing the great open fields and old common land. This many of them did, migrating to the towns to begin a new and alien way of life to them.

Along with other places, there were hardships in Trumpington. For instance, while the private bill for enclosure of the parish was being formulated, the agent wrote a letter. "Old A. . . . says he won't sign the Bill unless he gets his 7 acres."

And old A. . . . must have got them, as the Parish Enclosure Bill was passed in 1801.

The Reverend Mr Heckford kept a watchful eye on the events of the Enclosure Bill — and wrote his comments in the margin of the parish copy. Against the heading commencing—

> That as soon as conveniently may be after the said Commissions shall have finished the partitions and allotments of the lands intended to be divided and enclosed,

he writes —

> and a very indefinite term — for in this instance the Allotments were made at Michaelmas 1802 and the Award is still not made yet — 1806.

He comments on the exception from the Vicarage power to grant leases of twenty acres in the Hauxton Field saying "a necessary clause for the benefit of the next incumbent" and also on the direction that certain lands awarded to the Vicar should be fenced round with posts, quickset hedges and fences by the adjoining owners. With acerbity he writes —

> This is frequently shamefully executed — and where is the remedy?

Nor does he altogether approve of the way monies from a power of sale shall be distributed. His marginal note reads—

This is obligating a great power and the Commissioners frequently do not attend to this business, as it is frequently badly executed; had they permitted me to execute the clause I could have saved 25 per cent.

There is the impression that Parson Heckford was not too happy about the effects of the Act on the vicarage lands and glebes. He fairly seethes with anger over the clause that the Commissioners may direct the course of husbandry saying —

The utility of this clause is doubtful — at least it is often much abused or not properly applied; the Farmers even permitted in this instance to hoard up their dung for 2 years previous to allotments, to the great injury of the Tithe Allotments, which way, of course, it is impoverished — and no manure ready for it as in the other allotments. Nor do the Commissioners consider this in their compensation at all.

But even if he had to accept circumstances he could, and did, record his sentiments.

One of the Vicarage tithe dues that was swept away by the Enclosure Act was the right of the vicar to "twopence for smoak" from every chimney in the parish. The present incumbent would do quite nicely if this privilege still obtained.

But vigilant as Mr Heckford was on the parson's dues, he quite often had difficulty in getting them in. Church tithes had been a cause of major resentment in England for years. When Trumpington realised that under a completely new system here they were, still having to pay out something to the vicar, it was a most unpleasant shock. So parson could wait.

When his successor was in the vicarage, Mrs Heckford wrote him with a list of unpaid dues, saying that the debtors denied they owed the vicar anything "and quite rudely by the first two named."

Poor Mrs Heckford. Money was obviously not plentiful with her. She asked Mr Hailstone to support her application for a pension from a charitable source and pathetically added that she hoped he was enjoying living "in the place she once thought a paradise."

The Reverend John Hailstone took office in 1817. He lost little time after his induction in reminding his parishioners of their duty towards their vicar, for in April of that year he sent out a notice.

By the Enclosure Act Easter Offerings were reserved to the Vicars. Fourteen years have passed without any demand being made and the Vicar now leaves it to the Inhabitants to make what voluntary offerings they please.

His parishioners apparently were not overmuch pleased. They contributed the sum of 13s. 4d.

On the south wall of the Chancel in Trumpington Church are the Anstey memorials. In 1838 Christopher Anstey wrote to Mr Hailstone of "the warmest desire of myself and Family to erect some memorial to our departed Mother." This Christopher Anstey was the son of the man who had inherited the old Beaufoes Manor, renaming the manor house Anstey Hall, by which name it is still known today. Along with the rest of the polite world Christopher Anstey visited the fashionable watering place that was Bath. And what he saw there caused him to write a book, a satire called the New Bath Guide, gently ridiculing the habits and manners of the people who flocked to take the waters. Written in verse, it ran to several editions and was popular for quite a while. And it did at least earn him a final resting place among the poets in Westminster Abbey.

John Hailstone was vicar of Trumpington for thirty years. His view of Trumpington High Street would have been that it was a very busy road. As it was indeed, for it carried the traffic of two main roads to London. Not only wheeled, but four-footed as well as webbed. Cattle for the London market walked their way there. It is said that some of the oxen who had fallen lame on their journey were shod at the Trumpington smithy of John Nichols. He fitted them with a shoe made in two parts, one on either side of the cloven hoof.

Then, and earlier, travel to London presented no difficulty. There was a seven day a week service, with the mail coach giving a choice of either the Royston or Walden road. The fly held four passengers and did the journey from Cambridge to London in ten hours — weather and road permitting. Even if there were aching bones at the end of it, the journey was worth every penny of the 12s. it cost. For 10s. there was a choice of either a six or four-seater stage coach. But for real leisure and thrifty travel, best in summer, there were the stage waggons. With the goods forward and any passengers under cover of the tilt at the rear, the slow progress to London could have been very pleasant. While the waggons of Mr Burleigh and Mr Salmon inned at the *Black Bull* and the *Green Dragon* in Bishopsgate, those of Mr Gillam went straight to their destination, "the Cambridge warehouse next Great St Helen's" in the same street.

The last view of Mr Hailstone must be seen through the eyes of a small boy named Widnall, one of his congregation. The then elderly vicar was in the habit of levelling his quizzing glass at members of his flock as they entered through the church door and watching them progress to their seats. A habit which was quite unnerving to strangers.

Perhaps it is just as well that both the gravel pits are now no longer visible. For the Enclosure Act gave Trumpington parishioners the right to them for their own private use, as well as for making and repairing public roads and highways. The onus on the parish to repair the latter has gone, but free gravel for the digging could have been a useful amenity for today's garden paths.

Our village forbears left behind them "An Account of Common Day Work done upon the Roads" in 1738. Biting the end of his quill pen, the village scribe must have cast around much in his mind before hitting on the headline "Before we Began". And there, set down in the form of a small ledger, is the record of a community effort.

Ned Goodwin's cart, William Stacey's cart, the carts of John Spencer and John Hailes: William Impe — one load of stones. From March through to September they laboured, and every man's effort and contribution is carefully set down. "Stones delivered for common day's work half a load for a day" — three loads each from Richard Grain, James Harradine and Elias Bland.

Common day's work for all Jobbs —

to John Creek and John Newman 1½ days each for cleaning the swamp at the end of the town

to William Dobson 6 days for digging the swamp by Harradine's

To John and Richard Allen for digging 3 loads of gravel 1 day

There are other names, too, familiar either through their descendants or by their Georgian tombstones in the quiet green of the old churchyard. Marshall, Peters, Wilson, Headly, Haslop and Haggis.

Dig down far enough and some of those carted stones would still be found under the main Trumpington to Cambridge Road.

Compare today's values with those of yesterday, as they appear in the final bill.

Laid out in all upon the roads for the year 1738.

	£	s.	d.
204 days work of carts at 5d. per day	51	0	0
229½ days work of labourers at 9d.	8	12	1½
For digging 845 loads of gravel at 3d. a load	10	11	3
For ground where the gravel was dig	2	10	3
For gathering 116½ loads of stones at 1s. 6d. a load	8	14	9
For ditching, paling and other Jobbs	6	18	6
	£88	6	10½

And no tea breaks either.

There is rather a peeved footnote to the account which reads —

Towards which Trinity Hall paid only £10. The rest all done and paid by the parish.

To be fair to the college, the amount of its land in comparison with that of other landowners in the parish was very small indeed. But the grievance was there. Because there was no central highway authority, repair of the highways fell on the parishes. And inhabitants felt that these major roads were largely used by travellers from a distance. Like, for example, the college students. So they skimped, or left undone, the highway repairs.

The extensive reparations of 1738 were probably only carried out because deep ruts had made the road impassable to wheeled traffic. Only dire necessity could have moved Trumpington do anything so vigorous.

Things more actively connected with the parish were treated with greater expedition. In 1776, "a new Well Curbe" was fitted to the Town Well and "the lidd" was mended — all for 3s. 6d. Ditching at the brick bridge (this was probably at the boundary by Brooklands Avenue Cambridge) cost the parish 17s. 9d. with 2s. for "sinking the ford at the arch" and there was a charge of 1s. for "work at Town Plow".

But when the Parish Constable collected rent from the Widow Aunger and Henry Creake in that same year, he added an outgoing to the bill. He knew what it meant. Now only the Almighty does. For what today can be made of "Gave the Goly Gipes"?

And Then Victoria

REGARD for the monarchy was at a low ebb in 1837 when Victoria ascended the throne. There can certainly have been no inkling then in the minds of Trumpington mothers that fifty years later their daughters and granddaughters would be subscribing, with other women all over the country, towards a Jubilee present for that young girl from Kensington Palace. Probably the only people on whom her accession made an impact were the bell ringers. A little extra money is always useful. And for the parish clerks and constables it meant little more than altering "King" to "Queen".

John Nichols was the village blacksmith, a busy man in those days. His forge echoed not only to the sound of shoeing, but to requests for the making of household articles. For the "one new poker and two new locks and keys" he made to order in 1841 he charged the parish 3s. 6d. And just like that other village blacksmith he led the choir on Sundays in the church. Where, incidentally, at that time there was a singing gallery at the west end of the church and adepts on the violin and flute accompanied the singing.

In mediaeval England John Wycliffe and the Lollards were thorns in the side of ecclesiastical flesh. They questioned the tenets of the Church and wandering Lollard preachers gained support among many people.

But Nonconformity proper really started in the seventeenth century and the 1685 Visitation shows how, by then, the movement had taken root. Chatteris "abounded with Quakers"; there were many Dissenters at Orwell; Oakington was "the most scandalous parish and worst in ye diocese with a Fanatick Schoolmaster" and Trumpington had "one stiff Dissenter". The Dissenters held their meetings, or conventicles, in houses belonging to their sympathisers. On one occasion, at least, a conventicle was held in a barn, that of Thomas Cambridge in Trumpington. There was a considerable gathering of people

"400 or 500 as is sayd from several places". And these people had gathered together from surrounding towns and villages to hear the words of their preacher, a man named Smith, of Royston,

One of the great pastors of St Andrew's Baptist Church in Cambridge was Robert Robinson, who took over the ministry there in 1761. Money was not plentiful with the church and Robinson took to farming to augment his income. But his pastoral work went on and so did his writing. He had already produced several theological works, although the necessary books for research were not always easy to come by. However, at Trumpington he had two good friends, Ann and Susannah Calwell. They lived in a house belonging to Christopher Anstey and received permission from Dr Anstey for Robinson to have the use of his library for researching.

With the blessing of St Andrew's Baptist Church, now with a far greater membership than the thirty-two it had when Robinson took office, the Free Church in Alpha Terrace Trumpington was built and consecrated in 1899. The land on which the church is built was given by Stephen Mansfield. He lived in a house named Gilmerton that once stood on the corner where Long Road and Trumpington High Street meet.

In these Welfare State days of hospitalisation we can look wryly at a letter sent to the vicar in 1869 from Addenbrooke's Hospital in Cambridge. There had been a special church collection for the hospital which had raised the sum of six guineas. And this amounts, the writer said, entitled the parish council to recommend one in-patient and two out-patients . . . . for every two guineas to be transmitted. Less efficient than today? Oh, certainly. But much more human.

Highlight of 1887 was the Jubilee Celebrations. And here Trumpington exerted itself. It had to when it came to the Union Jack, because Cambridge had sold out of them. And so the Jack was hand-made in the village, to fly from the church tower on an improvised flagpole. There were all kinds of fun and jollity — like a leg of mutton atop a greasy pole, for instance — and, of course, there was the feast, for which the men filed into one tent and the women and children in another!

And the fare to celebrate those fifty golden years? This is it. Between them 626 people consumed 645 pounds of meat, 1000 rolls, 300 pounds of plum pudding, 200 tarts, 21 pounds cheese,

14 pounds biscuits, 14 pounds sweets and 24 of sugar; 6 gallons of milk, 3½ barrels of ale, 56 dozen bottles of ginger beer, soda water and lemonade; 5¾ hundredweight of ice, pickles and vinegar. With a very moderate pound's worth of tobacco and pipes to follow.

Pleasures were simple — for the cottagers. There was the Flower Show to which heightened interest was given one year by the addition of a bee tent. When the expert lost one swarm on the way to this tent, the interest must have been intense.

Those villagers for whom Venice was unheard of must have been quite surprised by the Venetian fete, especially in connection with the Trumpington Flower Show. But in the dark of a summer's evening, those fourteen boats with Chinese lanterns and coloured lights fore and aft must have been a pleasant sight as they slipped along Trumpington's stretch of river. Whether the glee singers in them were troubled by mosquitoes is not recorded.

The final incident in the decade, in the century — and in this history — is the story of Alphonse Thomas. One day in 1894 the body of a man was found near the Hauxton Bridge after the sound of gunshot had been heard. Nobody recognised him, either in Trumpington or nearabouts. But he had died in the parish. And so his body was reverently laid to rest in the then new churchyard on the corner of the Shelford and Hauxton roads. There was even a straggle of mourners to follow, either from pity or curiosity.

That was the start of the story. It carried on when the enquiries went abroad, until finally the facts emerged. The body was that of a young Frenchman who came from Dampierre in France. There he had been "a maker of sabots and was of an exemplary character." But why did this exemplary young man travel the distance he did — four hundred miles in two days — to die by his own hand in Trumpington?

The answer is as much a mystery now as it was then.

But then there are so many unanswered questions. For instance, Everard de Trumpington and King John. Everard was with the king's army at the siege of Carrick Fergus, near Ulster, in 1210; an unfortunate time for Hugh de Lacy who lost his castle in the event. Was it the Runnymede Charter of 1215 or the annulment of it by the Pope that severed Trumpington's allegiance to the king?

And what of Richard de Trumpington, husband of Meliandre? Outlawed for a felony in 1272, what happened to him? Perhaps the succession of Edward I in the same year ensured him a pardon and an ultimate burial in consecrated ground. For certainly a Sir Richard de Trumpington was recorded as being buried in Gorleston Church in Norfolk. Moreover, his coat of arms was the well-known one we see in the parish church at Trumpington.

Roger himself, the Crusader of 1270, left on unexplained journeys. In 1281 he was "passing beyond the seas with John de Vescy", and four years later was again overseas. But whether soldiering or on a pilgrimage — and the latter could last up to four years — is not known.

The boundaries of the ancient farm lands are impossible to define, but the names sound mellifluous on the ear. St Foin Close, Lordship Close, Old Mill Holt, King's Close, The Lawn, Seaby's Spinney, Camping Close, Feast Close and Fish Pond Close. With the people who knew them, all gone.

A fitting end to this history would be to write that the bells of Trumpington Church rang out the end of the old year, and of the nineteenth century, with a jubilant peal. So they may have done. But any knowledge on this is buried with the ringers in the church-yard: the records are silent too. So let it end as it began — with William de Warenne and the Caillis.

The Normandy town of Bellencombre headed the vast estates in both Normandy and England of William de Warenne, who fought with the Conquerer at Hastings. Fifteen kilometres south of Bellencombre lay the little village of Cailly; and from here would have set out that William who was to own, among other land, a considerable part of the village that came to be called Trumpington.

Across the time of nine centuries Trumpington still stands linked with that Cailly of old Normandy. For the remains of the Norman castle can still be found at Cailly today.

Authorities Consulted

Documents and records consulted at:—

Cambridge Shire Hall Archives.
British Museum.
Cambridge University Library.
Jesus College Archives.
Registry of Wills, Ely Consistory Court (Miss H. Peake)
The Trumpington Parish Church (The Vicar and Churchwardens)

Books consulted:—

Documents relating to Cambridgeshire Villages. W. M. Palmer and H. W. Saunders.
Trumpington Parish Records and Notes left by Rev. A. Moule.
Story of the Cambridge Baptists. Bernard Nutter.
The Man in the Pew. A. Tindal Hart.
Social History of England. G. M. Trevelyan.
Reminiscences of Trumpington. S. P. Widnall.
Archaeology of the Cambridge Region. Cyril Fox.
Loss of Normandy. F. N. Pawicke.
Bedford Victoria County History.
Ground Work of British History. Warner and Marten.

Photograph Acknowledgements

Mrs F. Andrews, the Reverend D. M. Maddox, Mrs L. Marshall, Miss A. M. Matthews, Mr S. J. Newell, Mrs J. Stubbings and Miss C. Willers.

A WHEELWRIGHT OF HOXNE

A Story of Country Life

by BETTY RUTTERFORD

Betty Rutterford (née Harrington) was born at Hove in 1916 and on leaving school she took up secretarial work. Whilst on holiday in Suffolk she met Aubrey Leggett, whom she married at Eye in 1941. They lived at Hoxne until 1961 when they moved to Stowmarket: they later moved again, this time to Ipswich. Aubrey Leggett died in 1969, and in 1970 his widow married Percy Rutterford.

Introduction

I have compiled this simple story of country life from information given me over the years by my late husband, Aubrey Leggett, who died in September 1969. I am most grateful to my sister-in-law, Mrs Una Green, and to my son David for their help with detail over some of the things remembered.

I have recorded these things in memory of Aubrey and his father, Herbert, their forebears and fellow craftsmen of whom I would mention, in particular, Hubert Baldry of Horham. General work can still be seen around the countryside in carts, waggons, wheels, gates and suchlike all in themselves memorials to their skill. At Hoxne the skill of my husband and his father is shown in the new wooden top to the Goldbrook Bridge constructed about 1911; new lychgates to the Parish Church copied from an old design and made by my husband which were consecrated by the Bishop in 1954 and the Coronation seats which he and Mr Baldock were commissioned to make and erect in Cross and Low Streets in 1953.

A Wheelwright of Hoxne

The Early Years.

IN ATTEMPTING to write of my life, a somewhat uneventful saga, it is only to record my impression of country life and in particular to tell of life as a wheelwright as it was when I was born.

I was born to Herbert and Eliza Leggett, a wheelwright and his wife, on 31st March 1895 at Hoxne in Suffolk. They christened me Aubrey after a forebear, a name that would have sounded better had there been a prefix of 'Sir'. As it was, the highest title to which I was to aspire was Most Noble Grand in the Order of Oddfellows and that was grand enough for me. My mother told me that I was born in a high wind, so high indeed that my birthday was unlikely to be forgotten quickly by the local community. The end of the Chapel at Pulham, a village not far from Hoxne, was blown in and the Minister was killed in his pulpit. In my own village the caravans were blown over at old Billy Keeble's Fair. Billy was a cheap-jack who sold china and glass around the villages during the week and held a fair on Saturday nights during which there was usually a singing competition in which the audience acted as judges. The winner received a copper kettle which, in those days, was not of any great value. Some Saturday nights for a change he would hold a hot plum pudding eating competition. For a small entrance fee competitors were given a plate of hot pudding and a spoon and the winner was the first to clear his plate. Again the prize was a copper kettle.

My sister Una was five years old when I was born and for as long as I can remember she always mothered me. As children we shared everything, even if it was only a single sweet it was divided in two. Even the simplest treats were not taken for granted then as they seem to be to-day. The bare necessities of life were often a luxury to some in those days. We grew up close to the wheelwright's workshop on whose bench each of the tools necessary for my father's trade had its own place and woebetide anyone who moved one from its rightful place. The bench and the space above it were sacred places but under that bench was a veritable wonderland. A tiger's head complete with teeth and glass eyes, a light wooden model of the first flying machine and hundreds of little things which, if one was not in the way, could be investigated to one's heart's content. It was a source of constant amazement as one never knew what would be unearthed next. The floor, which was swept once a week, was covered with shavings that came from father's work as a wheelwright, coffin maker or the other multifarious jobs which came the way of a country wheelwright. The whole place was much more fascinating to us children than the modern toyshop. Under that bench I well remember finding old almanacs and other literature including advertising leaflets and children's story booklets bearing such imprints as Mother Seagal's Syrup, Blue Cross Tea, Maypole Soap, Clarke's Buffalo Dog Cakes, Monkey Brand, Hudson's Soap and those of many other brands. With a little imagination our finds could well become an old dinosaur or perhaps a dragon. Imagination had to play an even bigger part then than it does to-day. Most children, no matter how poor their parents, had one or two toys but some of these were very crude. These required more imagination than usual and perhaps, as a result, their owners gained greater pleasure from them.

Inquisitive, like all children, from time to time we asked father what he was making and if it was a toy for us we could expect the answer that it was "a trunnell for a goose's eye". We came to accept this answer and did not question further to find out what this mysterious object might be. The same answer might be given to an unwelcome visitor who came to the workshop and later in life I used the same words to answer my own son's enquiries and those of others where I thought the words would serve.

I went to the village school when I was four and a half years old, staying there until I was fourteen whilst they tried to teach me the three Rs. I have few recollections of those early school days but I do remember that I used to repeat everything parrot-fashion following exactly what I believed the other children were saying. We used to say Grace and it was not until I could read that I found that my oft repeated "The Plague of Flies sent down from heaven" should have been "The Bread of Life sent down from heaven". I am sure that many others made similar errors through repeating misheard words. Before I left the village school my sister became a pupil teacher there. She also taught at two other schools in the district later, only leaving when she married.

Between the ages of fourteen and sixteen my parents sent me to the local Grammar School at Eye, which ancient foundation was eventually closed after several hundred years existence teaching children in 1965. After leaving school I went straight to work with my father until service with the Royal Navy during the First World War took me away from Hoxne. After the war there was insufficient work with my father to warrant my return to Suffolk so over the next four years I found employment as a bar attendant with my cousin in London and then as a coach builder. Gradually the work at home became more plentiful and I was able to return there to work.

Although from an early age I had watched my father at work and also had a set of small tools of my own I was still very fumble fisted when I began again to work with him. It was some time before my work remotely approached the high standards he set. Like all true craftsmen he was constantly striving after perfection and insisting that I should do likewise. Under his expert tuition and supervision I eventually became a fully fledged wheelwright. I have never been certain if I had become the third or fourth generation of wheelwrights in father's family, a family that had originally come from Kelsale and of which part had then moved to Laxfield where my father and his brothers and sisters had been born.

There was a strong dividing line between domestic and wheel-wright activities. All callers to see my father about his work came through the big gates and crossed the yard to the workshop. My mother only reckoned to open the house front door for callers on domestic or social matters. I well remember one old lady coming to our front door with a saw that needed sharpening. My mother from an upstairs window made it quite clear that she was not coming down to attend to such matters and indicated that the saw should be taken direct to the workshop. The poor old soul was so taken aback by all this that she replied, "What, are you too high to come to your front door?"

A Wheelwright's Work.

We had to have a steady supply of timber for our work and this we just could not go out and buy when we needed it. All the wood we were likely to need had to stand in the yard for a year before it could even be cut up. It then had to stand for between three and five years more to season. This meant that there was capital which laid 'dead' for up to six years — a fact that my mother constantly bemoaned but one that was inevitable.

My father usually bought elm, ash and oak trees that had been cut down on farms during the winter. These were brought to our yard on a transporter known as a 'Jim'. This consisted of two very strong high wheels, usually about 6 foot 6 inches in diameter, running on steel arms which were mounted in an arched axle bed allowing about 3 foot 6 inches to 4 foot clearance from the ground. Fixed on top of the axle bed was a pole about 6 inches square and some 10 to 12 feet long. At the axle end of the pole was a very strong forged hook and at the other end an equally strong shackle. The first job was to lever the tree off the ground and place a wooden roller under it so that it was balanced like a see-saw. The 'Jim' was now man-handled into position over the tree with a wheel either side of it and a chain was placed under the tree at the end which now lay at the axle end. The pole was now pushed to a practically vertical position and one end of the chain was hooked over the hook. It was now necessary to pull the other end of the chain taut and place that also over the hook. Now with a rope or chain previously attached to the shackle end the pole had to be pulled down to lie along the tree and another chain had to be put under the tree to attach it to the pole at the shackle end. By getting the pole into a horizontal position the tree was held clear of the ground and all that was necessary was to attach the horses' traces to the shackle and get them to haul it to the yard. In a shady place in the yard the procedure was reversed and the trunk was deposited to remain for a year before it moved one step nearer to being used in the workshop. The following year the trunk was rolled to the edge of the saw-pit where it was stripped of its bark and generally smoothed up with a draw knife. Now a chalk line had to be snapped vertically on each end and this was usually in the centre of the pith. The chalk line was then held and lines then snapped from the two upright lines at each end along the length of the tree. To those unaware of this method of drawing lines perhaps a word of explanation would not come amiss. A length of string is covered with chalk by rubbing the chalk back and forth along the the string. Now if the string is held taut between the two end marks and it is lifted in the middle and then allowed to spring back a straight chalk line is deposited on the trunk joining those two end marks. These lines were the guide from which we measured the thickness of the planks or boards we would require. When the trunk was marked up one side it had to be rolled over and marked on the other before being moved to the centre of the saw-pit. The saw-pit, now thank goodness a piece of torture that is no longer in use, had one man in the pit and another on the platform above. Each had a handle of a very large saw with which they sweated many a long hour sawing the trunk into planks. These planks were stacked with thin splines between them to let the air circulate and there they remained for three, four or even five years to season. It was really hard work and was called 'dead horse' because of the time the results had to lie idle before being used. Whilst working one end of the saw I often recalled how as children the saw-pit had been a playground. Father used to put us down the pit with bucket and spade to play and he also provided us with a little pump and a well so that we could pump water to mix with the sawdust to make pies. To me sawdust was more fun than sand in those days.

The making of a wheel was a long hard job, especially on those for farm tumbrils and wagons. First came the making of the hub from big and heavy lumps cut from trees which had been previously cut, stored and dried. The spokes were then made with a spoke shave and each spoke held in a vice whilst it was shaped. The big felloes had to be sawn and then cut out with an adze. Each wheel was made from templates, all of which were kept in the workshop each marked with the name of the owner from whom the wheel had come. When the wheel was finished it had to be trundled by hand up the road some two hundred yards to the blacksmith. A wheelwright must work very closely with the blacksmith and my father and I were very lucky to have good ones, several in their turns, in the village to do work for us. Shoeing or rimming was the process by which the blacksmith put on an iron rim all round the felloes and the skill with which this was done made all the difference to our finished work. The rim was heated before being put on and was then cooled with water to shrink it on to the felloes. This was an extremely skilled job requiring great accuracy and the sweat would run from our faces whilst helping with this process.

There was one blacksmith's apprentice about whom I recall two stories. One day whilst a horse was being shod the youth, using both hands, had his mouth full of nails. Due to some cause the lad swallowed a nail and somewhat alarmed told his master only to be reassured by, "That's alright boy, there's plenty more in the tin". On another occasion the lad was making bill hooks and omitted to weld on the steel edge to the wrought iron blade, thus making them useless. When he mention this fact to his master he was told, "Never mind boy, we've got our name up!"

Hubert Baldry was a colleague, friend and very skilful and ingenious craftsman. He lived at Horham about three miles from Hoxne and kept the *Dragon Inn* there which had been in his family for nearly two hundred years and closed soon after his death in 1965. With the *Dragon* went a wheelwright's shop and he also ran a taxi business. If one of us were hard pushed over an undertaking job or other work he would help out and lend a hand. During the Second World War in order to get from Hoxne to Horham meant that Horham Aerodrome had to be crossed and this was then in use by the American Air Force who flew from there their large Flying Fortresses. Without crossing this airfield getting to Horham meant a detour of between a mile or two around Stradbroke which was quite unthinkable owing to petrol rationing. A visit to the Provost Marshal at the American Base resulted in a pass being issued allowing me to cross the airfield on business trips to Horham as and when the occasion arose. So that my wife could accompany me on such trips I had to register her as an Undertaker's Assistant and after the war I kept these passes for their interest value.

Wheelwright's work, as I knew it, included all types of carpentry, painting and other jobs in building work as well as undertaking. When I was working with my father neither of us would ever dream of planing coffin boards in advance although this would have saved a lot of time and hard work when they came to be needed. We would also have been able to do this when we were slack. Many is the time we have had to work right through the night to get a coffin finished in time. Still, preparations in advance could not be done because we would have been, to use a good old local expression, "cried shame of" for preparing for anyone to die. Later we did get round to buying coffin board partly prepared. Country folk could not accept the fact that in big towns coffins were kept ready and what is more often were displayed in undertaker's windows. I must admit that I had been shocked as a child to see a coffin in a window.

There was a lot to think about in a local business in order that one did not cause offence. We had a pear tree and I was sent to take some lovely ripe pears to an old man as a gift. He thanked me and accepted the pears but told me to tell my father that he hoped he would not be requiring a coffin just yet. This sort of attitude also prevented us enquiring after anyone who was ill lest they should think we had some ulterior motive for making the enquiry. There was however a bricklayer we knew who was taken ill with consumption and knew he was going to die. His wife used to wheel him round to the workshop regularly and he would craze my father and his wife to have his coffin made so that he might see it made ready. Eventually, getting tired of the constant visits, my father agreed to make the coffin and when it was ready he took it round to the old man's house. Not long after that he had to call again and collect the coffin as the old man had grown scared of the constant reminder of death but later, when his time came, he was buried in it.

Once after a funeral I had to take a covered wheeled bier pulled by a pony down the road, leading the pony by its reins. Suddenly it came on to rain very hard so I got inside and laid flat in the bottom of the bier and drove the pony that way. Whilst I could see out those outside could not see in. I shall never forget the look on the face of a man I knew well who thought he was seeing a ghost, the pony and hearse seemingly being driven by nobody. He did not stop to investigate, in fact he was not in a fit state to do so as he fell backwards into the ditch in his agitation, poor fellow.

It was in 1911 when we made and fixed new wooden sides to the Goldbrook Bridge. Whilst work was in progress we had to show a lantern to make it safe for anyone passing over the bridge. My father and I took turns, he spending the whole night on the bridge one night and I the next. Alone on the bridge in the middle of the night recalling the legend of how St Edmund had been betrayed by the glint of his spurs whilst hiding under the bridge I was able to conjure up all kinds of imaginary things. I was glad it was not for many nights we had to perform our lonely vigil as I felt the place to be distinctly eerie.

A Matter of Money.

Money was hard to come by and there were many with large families and lower incomes than ours. Often father and I did jobs for villagers for nothing or in exchange for produce such as eggs and vegetables. On one occasion we received a barrel organ in part payment of an outstanding debt. We could not afford to do things like this, but there it was we did it, and basically I feel sure we never felt any regrets afterwards although I must admit mother was rarely told of such deals. The greatest difficulty arose when the bills came in from the timber and iron merchants which had to be paid lest our necessary supplies dried up. At these times we would sometimes be out a whole day trying to collect outstanding debts, with little or no success, and returning home very little the richer and none the wiser. It was often the people best able to pay that kept us waiting for our money and in addition they had an irritating habit of knocking off the odd shillings and pence when at last they did pay. This we considered a mean practice since we only charged for time and materials used and could not afford to allow such discounts. To have offended them would have resulted in us losing other trade so we were stuck with them and had to swallow our pride at times and accept half a loaf as being better than no bread at all. One particular instance remains firmly fixed in my memory. I collected a lantern from a lady of considerable means, spent over an hour repairing it and then took it back to her. I charged one shilling (5p) and she kept me waiting a half hour whilst she collected up this large sum. Eventually I received the exact sum in halfpennies and farthings and she made sure that there was not a mite over. I resolved then and there to allow for this time wasted in future dealings with this lady.

With workshop premises our rates were higher than those we could expect just for a domestic dwelling and from time to time we had tools to renew. Inevitably therefore it was necessary for us to earn a few shillings a week more than the average farm worker or general labourer and this showed how very low were their wages as what we earned was little enough. In times of trouble we did not then have the social services as we know them to-day to fall back upon and there was much more self help, particularly in the rural areas. Some examples from our work books from 1929 onwards will give an example of the low wages earned even by craftsmen. In 1929 our hourly wage was one shilling an hour which had increased to three shillings an hour by 1949 and to four shillings and sixpence by 1960 when I ceased full employment to become one of the nation's retired pensioners.

	£	s.	d.

1929.   **For Farmer "A"**

May.

Self & son 1½ hrs. each repairing granary steps & landing . .   3. 0.

Wood & nails for same . .   4. 6.

9. new spokes to tumbril wheel & 6 new felloes for same . .   1. 10. 0.

Painting gate 2nd time. 3 hrs. .   4. 8.
(2½ lbs. paint 1/8d. included in the 4/8d.)*

*We made our own with pestle & mortar with red or white lead base.

     £2. 2. 2.

1929.   **For Farmer "R"**

Mar. 29th

Sharpening & setting cross cut saw -6 ft. saw. . . .   2. 0.

April 5th

Repairing side to tumbril & fixing trap stick . . . .   16. 0.

" 8th

New harrow pulling tree 9 ft. 4".   8. 6.

     £1. 6. 6.

1929.   **For Farmer "G"**

June 10th

Repairing black wagon, splicing pole & hind bit . . .   12. 0.

2 new ledgers to ladder . .   3. 0.

June 12th

Making harrow pulling tree . .   4. 0.

One new whipple tree . . .   2. 0.

July 2nd

½ pint turps & ½ pint Linseed oil   10.

" 17th

Splicing water cart shaft . .   2. 0.

Aug. 16th

2nd hand axle & boxes to box cart   10. 0.

Boxing wheels & fitting up axle .   4. 0.

Pareing off wheels & painting rims   6. 6.

Aug. 23rd

Castors 2nd hand for chair . .   1. 0.

		£	s.	d.
Sept. 9th	Rimming Turnip cart wheels & 6 new spokes to same & cleaning & painting same			
	14.felloes @ 4/- per felloe .	2.	16.	0.
	6.spokes @ 2/- per spoke . .		12.	0.
	Cleaning & painting wheels .		8.	0.
Sept. 25th	New shaft to Road wagon . .		14.	0.
		£6.	15.	4.

1930.
March 21st & 31st	Repairing Lamps at St. Edmunds Hall, Hoxne.			
	60.ft Copper wire & 4 knots sash cord.		14.	6.
	Labour		5.	0.
	Labour		8.	0.
		£1.	7.	6.

1933.
	For local Estate Agent.			
	Sign Board 4' x 20" . . .		4.	0.
	Writing same 84 letters . .		16.	0.
	Taking same to Diss & fixing .		5.	0.
		£1.	5.	0.

1933.
	For Mr B. Eye.			
	New Wheel to trap . . .	1.	2.	0.
	Repairing "What Not" & chair .		12.	6.
		£1.	14.	6.

1940.
Sept.	*Mr Brewer (Policeman)* Painting & lettering 6 steel hats for A. R. P. Wardens . .		6.	0.
1942.	Repairing window broken by military gunfire . . .		4.	6.

On the undertaking side of the business oak was becoming more popular than the cheaper elm for coffins, although most ordinary people still had, of necessity, to settle for elm. The last funeral I conducted with an elm coffin I had made in 1956 brought the funeral costs to a total of £22. 2. 6d. The last funeral I conducted with an oak coffin in 1960 with all the rising costs then came to a total of £30. 18. 6d. Compare these prices with two funerals, one in which elm was used and the other in which oak was used, which we recorded in 1929.

		£	s.	d.
1929.	Elm coffin	4.	10.	0.
	2 yds. of best wadding . .		2.	0.
	4 Bearers @ 4/- each . . .		16.	0.
	Church expenses with Hearse .		18.	6.
	Collecting bearers & arringin			
	funeral		5.	0.
	Pony & man for hearse . .		3.	6.
		£6.	15.	0.

		£	s.	d.
1929.				
April.	Best Oak Coffin with Brass furn-			
	iture and shroud in cotton			
	wool	9.	0.	0.
	Attendance at funeral . . .		5.	0.
	Church expenses	1.	5.	0.
	Man & pony for hearse . .		3.	6.
		£10.	13.	6.

Hoxne.

Start at the picturesque water mill, the low meadows and peaceful backwaters of the River Waveney. Work your way up the hill by the sides of fields to the nine oaks and Green Street. To the left lies Syleham with its Monks Hall, then Wingfield with its moated castle on the one road and with Stradbroke on another. To the right lies the Church and at the end of that short stretch of road turn right for Diss some six miles away passing through Oakley and Stuston. If however you turn right down the hill you come into Low Street and part of the main village of Hoxne with its old houses and cottages. The *Swan Inn* is in Low Street and when you have passed the inn you can turn right for Eye or left over the Goldbrook Bridge and on past St Edmund's Hall. Not far distant from this, in a field on the left, stands a stone memorial to St Edmund. Many are the legends surrounding this famous East Anglian King and Martyr who was later to find his resting place in the Abbey at Bury St Edmunds. Hoxne has its own legends for the monument is said to mark the spot where once grew an oak to which the King is said to have been tied by the Danes and shot to death with arrows. When after many hundreds of years this tree came down arrow heads were reputed to have been found embedded in the tree. Continuing from here up the hill past the council houses one comes to the Abbey and its farm to the right of which is an empty space where, until recently destroyed by fire, stood the old *Red Lion* Public House. Round the corner the third house on the right is where my family and I lived and at the end of the yard, away from the house, stood the workshops. This is Cross Street, the other main part of the village. Some two hundred yards past our house stands the blacksmith's shop at the junction of a road. To the right, along Nuttery Vale a junction is made with the Eye road again. However if you go straight on along Cross Street you will find the Baptist Chapel a short distance away and opposite it on the left is *Ye Olde Grapes Inn*. Further along still is Heckfield Green with its new council houses and bungalows and on past them is the village school. The road straight on from here leads to Stradbroke but if you turn right past the school you are on the road to the villages of Denham and Horham.

The village still has great charm and geographically has changed very little, if at all, during the sixty-six years it was my home. A few more new houses and bungalows have been built and some of the older ones have been pulled or have fallen down. The Parish Church and the Baptist Chapel still call the people to worship even if, as elsewhere, they do not appear to hear the call as well as they once did. In my young days practically everyone, unless he was an avowed heathen, attended regularly at some place of worship and both Parish Church and Baptist Chapel were always full. It was expected of the servants at the Hall, Oakley Park which was demolished many years ago, to attend church either in the morning or the evening with their master and mistress, but it was a case of a place for everyone and everyone in their place. The gentry sat in one part of the church and their servants in another. My father was at one time a member of the Plymouth Brethren but my mother, sister and I attended the Parish Church. I went first to Sunday School there and, as I grew older, to the morning and evening services. I was in the choir and also a bell ringer. I remember that I once stayed behind after choir practice and went up into the belfry only to find that the Church door had been locked on me. It was well over an hour before I was discovered and, not being very old at the time, I remember also how petrified I was there alone in the dark.

The character and characters of the village have altered a great deal. Years ago, when there was little or no traffic save the odd pony and cart, the public service consisted of a horse bus once a week on market day to take us the six miles to Diss but seats had to be booked in advance. As a result the village was much more of a community and from village shops, of which there were several, could be obtained almost everything for everyday needs. Bread, cakes, groceries, meat, ironmongery, boots, shoes, suits of clothing and drapery of all kinds and all doing reasonable business. It was quite an expense and something of an event to go shopping further afield. Travel difficulties also restricted courting so that families of the same village or nearby ones inter-married much more than they do to-day, so you would find a number of families of one name and all mostly closely or distantly related. We ourselves had no relations within nine miles of Hoxne. Generally speaking we were a happy community of some eight hundred odd people although we tended to be a trifle narrow-minded in the old days.

Looking through my Bible reminds me of the many biblical names once given to children. Some I can recall in Hoxne were Aaron, Abraham, Absalom, Amos, Bathsheba, Caleb, Ebenezer, Ephraim, Eli, Hagar, Hepzibah, Isaac, Jesse, Jonah, Levi, Moses, Naomi, Nathan, Obadiah, Ruth, Shadrach, Solomon, and Zephaniah.

Work in and around the village is almost entirely agricultural, or connected with it, such as the pipes made at the brickworks and used for drainage of the land. A clothing factory at Syleham, the next village in one direction, employs a number from Hoxne and more recently a mushroom factory has 'sprung up' between Hoxne and Horham. With the growing use of the motor car there are to-day many more people now living in the village whom one might, without any disrespect, once have called 'foreigners' — a term often even applied to people from the next village. To-day they are much more readily accepted into the community and indeed will have brought fresh life, ideas and interests with them. Village life has improved greatly since amenities like electricity, mains water and sewerage have become available.

Our toilet facilities were very primitive in the days before they were replaced by the Elsan closet in a shed near the back door and before the Elsan gave way to indoor flush sanitation, the ultimate refinement and something really worth asking guests in to have look at. Right across our yard was a double dweller or petty as we called it. This double dweller had on one side an adult's size seat and a child's size seat and on the other side of the dividing wall was another adult sized seat and this was the one I claimed as my own. When time permitted I would sit there sometimes for as long as half an hour puffing at my old pipe and finding myself getting more and more interested in the old newspapers which had been put in there as toilet paper. Somehow these had never seemed as interesting when they were indoors as reading matter. In winter with an old oil stove these newspapers and my spiders for company I was apt to forget time so I used to tell my wife where I was going so that at least someone had been informed of my whereabouts over the next half hour or so. She once looked into my side but beat a hasty retreat telling me I was very welcome to it with my pet spiders and its dark corners. Personally I used to find it very cosy. Never the less we were one of the first to put in an Elsan and one of the first to go on the main sewer when it arrived in the village. In spite of my finding the petty reasonably cosy I had always detested the necessary periodical emptying of the old closet.

Another link with the past was broken when the Dutch oven was taken out. It had been a good oven and the food which it had baked was as good as anything that could be produced in the new electric one, that was always assuming that the fire had been correctly stoked. The electric stove however had the great advantages of cleanliness and the ability readily to adjust the heat to that which was required. The box iron containing its heating material was a gem in its time but no one was sad to see that slung out and replaced by a chromium plated electric which, joy of joys, had a heat adjustment for various materials — gone was the hit and miss method of spitting on the base of the iron and guessing what the heat might be. The old copper which had heated all the water for the family wash and all our baths was also replaced by an electric one. The copper one however did duty for some time as a receptacle for the rain water collected from the roof. Water as soft as rain water was one of the joys of living in the country. Water tapped straight into the house was a great boon but it was so very hard in comparison with the water we had previously fetched daily from the pump two hundred yards away up the road.

Last but not least of the gifts electricity bestowed upon us was the electric blanket. It was so easy to switch on and so cosy and warm in our bed. This had replaced the hard though wonderfully heat retaining brick. I well recall the old ritual of brick warming on winter nights gone-by. Specially selected bricks, their number dependant on the number of beds to be warmed, were put before a clear fire about an hour before retiring. The bricks had to be turned so that the heat got right through and then tested by spitting on them to make sure they were not too hot and likely to burn the bed. They were then wrapped in brown paper and tied up with string ready to be popped between the sheets. I wonder if to-day people would be able to tear themselves away from the television long enough to attend to such matters. But there again it is all so difficult to remember how we used to read or write love letters upstairs by the light of a single candle. Now we just flick a switch and we have instant light and take it all so much for granted. It seems ridiculous to think that in my youth all the things that electricity has brought us seemed as unreal and as impossible as the thought that a man might go to the moon. I often think that in my life time we have had to adapt to more changes than any generation before us or for that matter any following generations are ever likely to have to cope with ahead.

Pastimes and Entertainment.

Each day after school my sister and I were given a task to perform for our mother and father which took about half an hour. After that we were free to play. I could boast of being quite popular amongst my friends as for a penny I would make a spinning top on my father's lathe, pounding away at the treadle with my feet. My friends were very discerning and for their penny, a vast sum in those days, they would spend several minutes deciding which was the best value for money. This little activity not only gave me pleasure but also provided me with pocket money. The wood used to make the tops came from pieces of 'wrongs' of which my father used to buy loads from farm workers who were allowed to sell them after they had cut down the hedges. 'Wrongs' were thick pieces of sapling, elm or ash, which had got out of hand and had to be cut down. My father used the wood for making sails for horse's collars.

My father made us a sledge and my first bicycle, a wooden penny farthing and there was a doll's house for my sister as well as a number of other substantially built wooden toys. We had to take care of these and some of them are still about in good condition. We each had hoops and mine was an iron one which I trundled along with an iron crome. Girls had wooden hoops which they bowled along with a wooden stick. My sister's was exceptionally large and she could skip through it throwing it over her head like a rope. There were of course skipping ropes and some had handles with little bells attached and others were simply a length of ordinary rope or linen line.

Good Friday heralded, for both men and boys, the start of the marble season and this used to be played in the street.

I used to like going to Green Ditch, a pond just down the road. The local boys used to fish in it during the summer but I preferred to slide on it when it had frozen hard enough in the winter. Water had a fatal fascination for me and I nearly came to grief as a result on many occasions. On the Abbey Pond I remember a boy did fall through the ice. Being small at the time and having had read to me a story from a little book I recalled the words from it, "Tom fell in the pond — but Tom got out again". Thus I was not unduly alarmed by events and stood idly by to watch him get out again. Fortunately aid was at hand and the boy was rescued. On one occasion I got wet by falling in at the edge of the pond and went home with my clothes frozen to me. I had to be thawed out in front of the fire and watched a small puddle take shape at my feet.

I used to enjoy going down to the River Waveney and diving in and swimming at a spot known as The Sailor's Hole. Here the water was very deep and local legend had it that the place was named after a sailor who had drowned there many years before. My frequent trips to the river used to worry my mother and eventually, when I was about twelve, she hid my bright red swimsuit. I searched for it every-where without success but the loss of a little thing like a swimsuit did not deter me from going to the river. I used to slip off across the fields and, if there were only other boys about, slip out of my clothes leaving them near the bank before diving in to swim in the nude. On one occasion I got cut off from my clothes by a bull and had to make a run for it to climb a tree without a stitch on. Luckily there was someone about who drove off the bull, allowed me to leave the tree and get to my clothes. I was glad I was not in my red swimsuit.

There was the occasion when I went out to play in my new breeches knowing full well that I should have changed before going out. Inevitably the breeches got torn and too frightened to go home I called on a kind lady I knew. She put some stitches in the tear and it was not until I got home that I discovered that she had sewn my breeches to my sock. I was now in quite a predicament for if I cut the stitches my sin would be discovered and if I left them in it seemed I would have to wear that sock indefinitely. I decided to keep the stitches in and hope for the best. I did not get away with it for long as within a short time my mother was demanding my socks for washing. I often wonder if the tanning I got would have been so great if I had owned up right away instead of waiting to be found out.

Each year, in the Village Hall, we had a treat in the form of a Magic Lantern show after which we were all given a bun and an orange. The pictures shown varied little year from year yet all might as well have been new as far as we were concerned. The particular ones we always looked forward to were of an old man in bed. He had his mouth open and a small mouse ran up him into his mouth and came out of his feet and then back up his body into his mouth. Another I remember was a pretty coloured sort of star that revolved. The smell of buns, oranges and paraffin oil pervaded the hall but this simple pleasure was looked forward to with considerable anticipation each year.

In my youth a German Band used to visit the village. This consisted of about a dozen players each in a smart uniform who were considered good and the tunes they played were very lively. We always looked forward to their coming although it was not possible to hold a conversation with them as they did not speak English. Another entertainment which we enjoyed for a time was the man, probably a Russian, who used to arrive leading a bear. The bear was muzzled and the man made a peculiar sort of singing sound to which the bear was supposed to dance. He did this by just 'pampling' from one hind foot onto the other. Perhaps I should explain that 'pampling' was the Suffolk word we used to describe 'just shuffling about'. I seem to think that we were more nervous of the man than the bear. In some book we read that the bear was taught to do his so-called dancing act by being made to stand on his hind legs on a very hot plate and so learnt to lift them in turn to escape the pain of the heat. We never found out if this was true or not but all I do know is that it spoilt the enjoyment of the turn for us. The man and bear used to sleep together in the stable at the public house and be out on the street by eight a.m. at the latest.

Another visitor who came fairly often was a German with a Barrel Organ, or Hurdy Gurdy, who had whiskers and appeared to us to be an old man. He carried this organ on his back and when he played it he propped it up on a single leg like a broom stick and turned the handle. We children liked to get close in particular to look at the pretty picture of a baby on the front of the organ. He did not like us to get too close and it seemed to us that if we did he swore at us in German. We could well have been wrong and the words have been ordinary words spoken in anger. Sometime before the First World War he came to my father's workshop and was, if I recollect correctly, selling cottons and tapes at the time. He told my father that he had worn a hole in his back from carrying the organ over all those years. At one time he had a monkey with the organ which wore a little red suit and matching red hat which it used to hold out for money. This monkey, which eventually died, was carried from place to place inside the man's jacket and if we were lucky it would shake little cold hands with us. There were two men with a heavy wheeled Barrel Organ similar to the one we once received in part payment of a debt. They pushed and pulled this heavy and awkward organ around and since both were disabled, one had a wooden leg, this called for quite considerable effort on their part. They were a part of the forgotten disabled men from the Boer War. We always used to dance in the street to their music and made sure that we had something to give them. Another man with a donkey drawn barrel organ also used to appear from time to time. Then there was the two Italian women who came with an organ and two love birds who for a copper paid to the women would pick a card from a pack on which would be written your fortune.

Certainly we seemed to suffer no shortage of wandering musicians and bands in our village and all added a little spice and variety to our lives. At such tender age we enjoyed the entertainment but gave no thought to the lot of the entertainers. The pittance we were able to offer must have seemed poor com-

(i)   Aubrey Leggett whilst in the Navy during the First World War.

(ii)   Una, sister of Aubrey Leggett and now Mrs Green, photographed during the First World War

(iii)   A family group. On the left Aubrey stands next to his father, Herbert, whilst his wife,
Betty, now Mrs Rutterford, stands with his mother, Eliza.

(iv)   Aubrey Leggett photographed by the River Waveney at Hoxne in 1957.

(v) Aubrey and Una Leggett, sixth and seventh from left of second row from front, in a school photograph taken in 1900.

(vi) Herbert Leggett and his apprentices at his Hoxne wheelwright's shop.

(vii)   The old *Red Lion* at Hoxne which was burnt down.

(viii)   Low Street, Hoxne, photographed before the First World War.

(ix) Aubrey and Una in about 1902 with toys made by their father, Herbert. The dolls' house is still in existence.

(x) Aubrey and Betty's son David in a horse and cart made by Aubrey.

(xi)   The showman's and modern caravan made by Aubrey.

(xii)   Chair-O-planes, made by Aubrey, in Cross Street meadow, Hoxne.

(xiii)   The lychgate at Hoxne Church for which, in 1954, Aubrey made this new set of gates.

pensation for their lack of permanent residence and the need to sleep rough at what ever place night should overtake them.

We talk about the youth of to-day as if they invented all the unpleasant things for which they get blamed. A bunch of youths in our village formed what became known as the Rough Band. Equipped with old cans, saucepans, tin dustpans and similar objects which made a racket when beaten they achieved an evil reputation. They would play their 'instruments' outside the houses of those they considered of low intelligence and thus worthy of their scorn and to annoy those whom they disapproved or who had annoyed them. Newly weds, where they considered the bride had not been all she should have been before her marriage, became a target for the band. These young roughs would continue with the din to the annoyance of victim and the neighbours until they were given enough money to take them off to the local. A type of blackmail that was deplored by all right-minded villagers.

My father was always happy with any piece of wood and often cut pieces from the hedgerow. These he would fashion into any-thing that took his fancy. Happy hours he spent whittling away before the fire in winter using his imagination and skill to turn the most humble piece of wood or stick into little people or animals. I kept all these little treasures he made over the years in a special cabinet which he had also made.

Whilst my father played the accordian he and my mother some-times sang songs to while away the long winter evenings. We also used to listen to the old hand wound gramophone playing records of the stars of the day such as Harry Lauder and Marie Lloyd. I honestly believe they gave us as much pleasure as the youth to-day get from their pop records but must admit the old horn on the gramophone was quite incapable of producing the volume of sound that children seem to need nowadays.

Personal Recollections

It seems strange to me now as I sit, in my latter years, lazily by the fire in winter or in a deckchair in the sun in summer telling these little stories to my wife to recall that my sister and I were once amongst the leading lights of the village. Certainly this is true regarding concerts, whist drives, dances and similar entertainment. I used to sing comic songs whilst my sister accompanied me on the piano — she also played for dancing. Others in the village provided different acts and local "dos" were always well attended. We also got well known outside the village and would get requests to help out at their concerts, fetes and the like, usually being provided with transport and refreshments but there were occasions when we were offered a small fee.

One thing that gave me much pleasure was building equipment similar to that used in Fairs, a subject that interested me all my life. I made many sets of plans and succeeded eventually in making a junior set of Chair-o-planes complete with decorated top and tarpaulin cover. This set was in great demand at fetes for many years but since it took up a great deal of space in the yard I finally sold it to a fair which came to the district. I have also made, for my own amusement and interest, swinging boats and two caravans, one of which was of the showman type. My family had several holidays in these caravans by the sea and I let them during the summer months and this paid for our holiday. They also supplemented my income to a small extent but the cost of getting them to and from the seaside and ever-rising site rentals made it progressively less of an economic proposition. The fact that I was to move from the country meant that I could not keep them anyway so I sold them to friends.

On our first wedding anniversary my wife and I cycled to Mendham and there hired a small rowing boat and spent a very pleasant afternoon on the river. After that I built my own flat bottomed rowing boat and oars for our own use. I also lent it to anyone else who asked when I was down at the river at Hoxne. It had other uses and I was several times called to rescue people stranded in Low Street near the *Swan Inn* where the road would get flooded for some distance and at times quite deeply when the river rose. Once I was called in a hurry and in my haste to get out the 'lifeboat' forgot that I had my few months old son in my arms. He fell off the chair head over heels onto the floor but fortunately he was more scared than hurt. No doubt I would have sung to him on my return as usual and in all probability it would have been one of my favourites,

> Come to tea on Sunday night,
> Winkles and water cresses,
> A nice little girl to sit on your knee,
> Winkles and water cresses.

Pa's gone out, Ma's not in,
Cook she's gone to her nieces,
There's only the parrot and he won't talk,
Winkles and water cresses.

As he would not have understood the words it must have been the repetitive little tune that lulled him to sleep!

Village Characters.

There were several characters in our village, and one such was "Freddie", a crotchety old man disliked by many. In Hoxne he had an allotment which he cared for but neither would he let others see what he was doing nor would he exchange his produce, as was the custom, with his neighbours, which annoyed and upset them. The time came, one April, when his onions should have been showing through the ground, but, instead, all that appeared was a crop of weeds.

"An enemy hath done this!" he was heard to cry out. Indeed, a conspiracy had been afoot to teach him a lesson, though I doubt whether it sank home.

A hard-working and energetic neighbour of ours was Mrs Boxer, a nickname given probably on account of her threatening attitude, who kept both her house and her many children spotlessly clean. As her husband worked on the land, there was little coming in for the large family, so she took a job at a big house in a neighbouring village where she did the family "wash". It was 5.00 a.m. on Monday mornings that she left Hoxne for Stuston and walked the five miles to do her work for which she was paid 1s. (5p) with food. It is little wonder that she was ill-tempered being so overworked most of the time. When upset, she would get into an argument which always ended up with, "I'll send you a bit of paper," (meaning a summons) and she patted her bottom at them and would say, "Talk to that". Mrs Figger was another of our neighbours. She was a poor, harmless old dear who, in her latter days, had hallucinations about a village man sitting on her bed or on her chest of drawers drinking a cup of tea and refusing to go away. Whenever this happened either she or her daughter-in-law would come around to request that I make the figure disappear. Whether I was at home or out, I would hasten to Mrs Figger's as soon as I heard about it and would say to the apparition, "Begone you bad old man," with which he would vanish miraculously.

"Thank you so much, Aubrey," Mrs F. would say, "that was good of you, now I shall be alright." — until the next time!

"Brethy" was a character who came into prominence each Whit Monday. On that day the Oddfellows had a Church Parade and Band with sports in the afternoon while in the Park there was a fair. Brethy used to wander among the stalls and swings at the fair selling winkles and oranges from the baskets he held on either arm, calling out, "Penny Wink Wink Wink," to draw custom. Pins were supplied so that the winkles could be picked out as the customers walked along, but he sold so many shells that were empty that it was said he ate many himself, placing the empty shells back in his basket.

So life went on much the same every day. Working hours were long but never boring and great satisfaction was drawn from it. Leisure time was short but full use was made of it. Machinery replaced wheelwrighting by hand many years ago, but I am proud to be included in that select band of craftsmen whose profession has almost died out. In the latter working years, this group had to turn their hand to anything in the carpentry, painting and small building line. I have repaired and made things of forms and features so odd that I cannot have failed at some time or other to have produced that mysterious object, "a trunnell for a goose's eye."

CULFORD HALL

Near Bury St. Edmunds

by GERTRUDE STOREY

Gertrude Storey (née Appleby) was born and educated in Scarborough. She later studied speech training and drama and in 1934 was a Gold Medallist at the London Academy of Music and Dramatic Art. In 1937 she married Dr Christopher Storey who, for twenty years before his retirement, was headmaster of Culford School, which is housed in Culford Hall, the subject of Gertrude Storey's historical study.

Introduction

"MEMORANDUM, the ninth day of March in the yeare of Our Lord according to the computation of the Church of England, One thousand sixe hundred fifty and eight, I Dame Jane Bacon of Culford in the County of Suffolk late wife of Sir Nathaniel Bacon late of Culford aforesayd Knight of the Bath deceased and before the wife of Sir William Cornwallis late of Brome in the sayd County deceased, Doe ordeine and make this my last will and Testament in manner following, First I will my body shal be buried in Christian Buriall in the Chancell of the Parish Church of Culford aforesayd soe neere my sayd late husband Sir Nathaniel Bacon as may conveniently be, without any pomp or solemne funerall early in the morning and not in the night att which I desyre that a sermon maybe, and I will that a devout monument or Tombe if not made in my life be made for me in such manner as I have given directions to my Executors". . . .

These are the opening sentences of the will of Jane, Lady Bacon, which she dictated to her lawyers as she sat in her Elizabethan Hall at Culford, near Bury St Edmunds, three hundred years ago. It is a very long will covering eight pages of closely-written seventeenth century script, signed and sealed in her Ladyship's own hand, and concluding thus:

"In Witnesse whereof I have set my hand and seale to a labell put through and fixed on top of this my will and Testament written in eight sheets of paper, and my hand to the last sheete the day and yeare first above written.

J A Bacon

Signed sealed and published the day of the date first above written in the presence of

John Norridge
Tho. Nelson
William Bugg
Peter Bennett

Med: I Dame Jane Bacon this twenty eight day of March 1659 have perused this my last will and testament and upon due consideration and mature advisement had thereof do publish and confirm the same.
Witnesse my hand

J A Bacon.

In the presence of
John Norridge
Thomas Nelson
William Bugg
William Girlinge
Thomas Humphry
John Peete"

Lady Bacon's will, now in Lord Iveagh's collection of Cornwallis Papers, still bears the "labell put through and fixed to the top", and to those who are interested in the history of Culford it is a most enlightening document, whilst names which before were only names become the people who lived at Culford long ago. Dame Jane Bacon was one of the most interesting of those people, and her business-like management of the estate was the sole reason for her descendants, the Cornwallis family, being able to live at Culford so long. Her "devout monument or Tombe" can still be seen in the chancel of Culford Church, and many people, looking at this monument, with the effigies of her grandchildren around her and her son Nicholas lying at her feet, have wondered what was her story.

Since the story of Culford is to many people only vaguely known, it has seemed worthwhile to relate, without any pretence to scholarship, what has been gleaned in the past few years. This is the endeavour of the following pages.

Gertrude Storey,
Lakeside,
Oxford.
January, 1973.

The Beginnings

FOR as far back as historians and archaeologists have been able to trace, people have lived in the district which we now call "Culford". The village of Culford, whose inhabitants number some three hundred, lies about four and a half miles to the north of the market town of Bury St Edmunds, in that part of Suffolk called the Blackbourne Hundred. It is built on light, sandy soil, the same kind in fact as was found here long, long ago, when Prehistoric man camped on the heathland amongst the silver-birches, which have always grown in the area. The land had the same characteristics in those far-off days as there are now, lack of dense forest, dry, sandy soil, which was easy to work, and water close at hand. Moreover, the district bordered on the Breckland, a prosperous part of England in those times, and not far off was the Icknield Way, the ancient highway along which tribes moved to the northern parts of East Anglia, so that this was a convenient place for people to make settlements.

From the wealth of Prehistoric and other early remains which have been unearthed and still are being discovered, and no other area in England has provided more, we know that early man lived here. The number of stone and flint axe-heads which have been found in the gravel-pits of Culford and West Stow, adjoining, prove that the hunting tribes of the Stone Ages lodged here; and there were people living here in the Bronze Age. There is the large burial-mound three miles to the north of Culford known locally as the "Hill of Health", on the way to Culford Heath, believed to be the burial-place of some Bronze Age chieftain, certainly the grave of a person of importance. Owing to the difficulty of moving the large trees which now grow on it, this tumulus dating from a thousand years before Christ has not been excavated, but a smaller mound to the south west of Culford in a part of the estate known as Dixon's Covert, was recently dug by the Curator of Moyses's Hall in Bury St Edmunds and small fragments of Bronze Age pottery were found, and also fragments of Iron Age Pottery in the surrounding ditch.

It is probable that the people who lived in this district early in the first century were amongst those who rallied to the cause of Boadicea, when the people who at that time inhabited what is now Norfolk and Suffolk rose in bitter hatred against the way they, and particularly their Queen, had been subjugated by the tyrannical Roman conquerors, and marched in revolt against the great Roman encampment at Colchester. At first it seemed they might succeed, but in the end the rising was finally and brutally quelled.

Later, when the power of the Romans had weakened in its turn, East Anglia was over-run by invaders from Germany, the Anglo-Saxons, and from the many interesting relics which were unearthed when the Anglo-Saxon cemetery was discovered on West Stow Heath in 1851, it is known that this colourful, resourceful people, obviously with a love of finery and decoration from the many gold and silver ornaments, brooches, beads, rings and mirrors they left behind, settled in the area in large numbers.

It was the Anglo-Saxons who first began to make permanent settlements, or villages, though their houses were merely four mud or wattle walls with a thatched roof; these were the ancestors of the people of Culford, and it was their descendants who lived here at the time of the Doomsday Survey, which is the first known official record of the district.

Culford is described in Doomsday Book as "Culeforda", which came from the Anglo-Saxon "Cula's ford." Who Cula was, no one knows, but he may have had some kind of dwelling, or farmed a strip of land, close by the stream which ran through Culford then at a place where it was possible to cross or "ford" it; the small settlement of huts in the vicinity gradually became known as Culeforda, or Culford, and so the village is known to this day.

The first landowner we hear of in connection with Culford is one Thurketel Dreing; how he acquired the manor, that is the estate of Culford, is not known; but in the British Museum is to be seen an ancient manuscript, a fourteenth century copy of the undated Anglo-Saxon charter, by which Thurketel granted Culeforda to the Abbey of Bury St Edmunds. Thurketel presented Wordwell, the next parish to Culford, to the monastery in 958, presumably about the same time as his presentation of Culford. This was a popular custom in those times, when the church held great sway over its members, and Thurketel gave Culford to the Benedictine Abbey, that the monks might say masses for the repose of his soul. It is recorded in Doomsday Book that the Abbot of Bury St Edmunds held at Culford, "1 carucate (a) of land. Always 2 villeins (b). And 2 bordars (c). Always 1 plough in demesne. Then one plough team belonging to the men, now half a team. And 8 acres of meadow. And 1 beast. And 2 hogs. And 85 sheep — And there are 18 soke-men (d) with half a carucate of land. Always 2 plough teams. These also belong to the Saint by sac and soke and all custome, nor could they ever give or sell without the Abbot's leave. Then valued at 4 pounds now at 3.

In the same township was a free-man with 1 carucate of land which Peter holds of the Abbot. 7 bordars (c). And 2 serfs (e). Always two plough teams, and a team of 2 oxen belonging to the men. 6 acres of meadow — then valued at 10 shillings now at 30. It is a league long, and 5 quarrantenes (f) broad. And pays in a gelt (g), 7¼d."*

Thus it was that by the time of William the Conqueror, the people of Culeforda had become an agricultural community, and a very hard-working community too, since they not only had to be self-supporting, but were obliged to work so many days in the week for the Lord of the Manor, the Abbot of St Edmundsbury. Indeed the "villeins" and "serfs" were almost as much a part of the possessions of the Abbot as the animals and stock which they tended, and they knew little else but work; the privileged tenants were not expected to perform such menial tasks as the villeins, but all had to toil while daylight lasted, ploughing the land with their ox-drawn wooden ploughs, sowing, reaping, threshing, grinding corn, and tending the sheep, which provided not only meat but wool for clothing. A great deal of barley was grown for brewing ale, rye-flour made their coarse bread, and oats, peas and beans formed a large part of the villagers' diet. The women worked on the land as well as the men, and when the day's work was done they must spin and weave the wool gathered from the sheep into rough home-spun tunics for their families, and into lengths of cloth for the monks at the Abbey, who regularly walked the dusty

*(a) As much as one team could plough in a year.
(b) The lowest class of tenants.
(c) Those who lived on the manor border land and paid no rent.
(d) Privileged tenants.
(e) Slaves.
(f) A furlong.
(g) A fine to the King.

road from St Edmundsbury to collect the Abbot's dues of grain, meat and wool.

Although there is no trace of it now, nor do we know who the incumbents were, there must certainly have been a Church at Culford in the twelfth century, as we find that Anselm, Abbot of the Monastery from 1119 to 1148, gave some lands in Hausted (Hawstead) which had belonged to Leveva, the late wife of Odo the Goldsmith, for the advowson of the Churches of Culford and Barton Mills, which were to pay a yearly rent of 40s., to the altar of St Edmunds. There is also a case on the Patent Rolls whereby a certain clerk, or cleric, named John de Salisbury, claimed that Richard the Abbot of St Edmunds, and others, had assaulted him at Culford in 1274 and broken his thighs and arms, and we may reasonably suppose that the unfortunate priest was none other than the cleric in charge of Culford Church.*

About this time Culford had the first of its Royal visits, for Edward I visited the Abbey of St Edmund, and Culford, on the 7th and 9th of February, in the ninth year of his reign, 1281; and in the twentieth year of his reign, following the death in 1290 of his Queen, the beautiful Eleanor of Castile, he spent a fortnight "betwixt St Edmunds and Culford, from the 27th of April".

Culford, often spelt "Culeford" by the time of the thirteenth, fourteenth and fifteenth centuries, had a very different aspect when Edward I visited it from the parish and estate we know today. The Church stood, almost certainly, on the same site as the present church, and there would be a house for the priest close at hand. Scattered around, but not too far off were the mud houses of the villagers, with the smith's forge, and simple stables for the horses; and there was, in all probability, a larger house, made of wood, and surrounded by a kind of palisade or fence, where the Lord of the Manor lived; for the Abbot of St Edmunds owned land in almost all of the Hundred of Blackbourne, and it was convenient to allow a Knight, or well-born person, to hold a manor in fee, or as a kind of tenant of the Abbot. The Lord of the Manor paid homage to the Abbot, farmed the land granted to him, and paid his dues regularly to the monastery, at the same time being in absolute control of the labourers on his land. In 1195 a certain Ralph de Mineres held half a Knight's fee in Culford, and it may

---

*(1) Pat. Rolls, 2 Edw III. pt. ii, 23 dg.

have been some descendant of his who was Lord when Edward I stayed in the parish. In any case, there must have been great preparation to receive the Royal visitor, and as he and his gorgeously-robed train cantered up the road from St Edmundsbury, little more than a dusty track, crossing the stream by the ford at the start of the village which still bore Cula's name, maybe the lord and his lady rode out to meet their Sire, and conducted him into the manor house, freshly strewn as it was with sweet-smelling rushes. To the peasants of Culford, dressed as they always were in tunics and hose, the older men in breeches, cross-gartered, and all of them in plain coarse wool, usually brown, the sight of so many elegant gowns as the King's company wore must have been surprising, the gentlemen in their velvet cloaks with hanging sleeves, and their brightly-coloured tights, the ladies wearing beautiful loose gowns trimmed with fur, and the King most resplendent of all in his ermine-lined mantle. Perhaps the magnificence and splendour to be seen amply repaid them for the extra labour involved in caring for the Royal guest, for extra labour there would certainly be, with the preparing and cooking of meals in the hot kitchens, the carrying of water for the nobility to wash, and wine and ale for them to drink.

It was May, and when the feasting was done, the pike, the boar's head, and the venison consumed, and the maids and serving-men were wearily longing for their hard beds, and the minstrel who had entertained the company with his songs had gone to rest, perhaps the King heard, in the dark stillness of the night, another song, a song which down the years has thrilled many a less exalted visitor to Culford, the voice of the nightingale fluting in the woodland around; and who can say if possibly for a time he forgot the cares of government and kingship, and thought only of the beautiful Eleanor, and imagined she was with him still?

Shortly after this, Edward again visited St Edmundsbury and held a parliament there with the object of obtaining further financial assistance. The monks refused to agree to the payment of a tax, and the King in great anger seized all the lands and manors of the monastery, collecting the revenues for a period of two years, until the Abbot relented. But at the time of his visit to Culford relations with the monastery were peaceful, and so we may believe the King slept well.

2 Rectors of Culford and Parishioners in the Fourteenth and Fifteenth Centuries

ONE of the few historians who mention Culford Church in their writings, Olive Cooke in *Breckland,* has described how one approaches the Church along pathways fragrant with violets, and this is certainly so in springtime nowadays. It may even have been so when Edward I visited Culford, we do not know, we can only imagine the Church at the heart of the village as it undoubtedly was then. Nor do we know who was the Rector at that time; but the records state that in the year 1319 Roger de Saxham was instituted as Incumbent of Culford, and thereafter there is a complete list of priests to the present day.

Following Roger de Saxham was Joseph de la Snore, 1324, who had a short stay, for Roger de Bernyngham was also instituted in 1324. This Roger evidently had a curate to assist him, for in a Subsidy Return of 1327 "Robertus Clericus" figures as being liable for payment in a tax imposed by a Parliament which sat at Lincoln in order to raise money to wage war against Scotland.

Subsidy Return 1327
VILLATA DE CULFORDE.

De Galfrido Euerhee	iiii	De Godefrido filio Prepositi	x
” Alicia le Reue	ii	” Adam Heruy	ii
” Henrico filio Ade	xviii	” Henrico Acke	xii
” Henrico le Hockster	xii	” Willmo Corteys	xxii
” Adam Finch	ii	” Adam Aylwy	xii
” Petro filio Radulphi	xii	” Radulpho de Couhern	xii
” Willo de Cleye	vii	” Roberto Clerico	xii
” Thoma Blauat	x		
Prob.		Summa (etc.) xxviii	

Following Roger de Bernyngham was Robert de Holm in 1367, and Joseph de Donyington in 1368. Then in 1368 Sir Nicholas de Tamworth became Lord of the Manor, and in 1369 presented the living to William de Lovetoft, who was Rector until 1415 and was followed by Joseph Leder. Thereafter was Joseph Bennish (1452), Richard Morgan (1452), William Stoke (1454), Richard Fest (1459), Joseph Stevenson (1473), Roger Fyneux (1524), and Joseph Balkey (1524).

The year 1524 saw the people of Culford, as of every other town and village in England, taxed in order that Henry VIII might wage war against the French King, Francis I. For this purpose he required large sums of money, in the opinion of Cardinal Wolsey "no less than £800,000 to be raised in the fifth part of every man's goods and lands". Accordingly the tax was imposed and the village of "Culforde" appears in a Subsidy List for that year. Those who were sixteen, if their wages were not less than £1 per year, had to pay 4d., those who possessed movable goods valued between £2-£20, paid 6d. in each pound, those who had movable goods valued at £20 and over paid 1s. in each pound. It will be seen from the list printed below that there were only five people in Culford with any kind of possessions (apart from the clergy, Roger Fyneux and Joseph Balkey, and nobility who were taxed separately), the other twelve liable for payment were all in the £1 wages per year class. The village must have been very small

CULFORD

	s.	d.
Thomas Longe in movables £10	5.	0.
Henry Wynter in movables £10	5.	0.
Wylliam Rowmbelow in movables £5	2.	6.
Thomas Feltwell in movables £3	1.	6.
Alys Forset in movables £2	1.	0.
Martyn Forse in ocupacyon be yer £1		4.
Rychard Feltwelle in vages be yer £1		4.
Wylliam Feltwell in vages £1		4.
John Hornyngold in labor be yeer £1		4.
Richard Feste in labor £1		4.
Wylliam Sawer in labor £1		4.
George Ame in vages £1		4.
John Rokell in vages £1		4.
John Walkard in labor £1		4.
John Stan in vages £1		4.
Robert Coke in labor £1		4.
Robert Feste in labor £1		4.
Summa.	19.	0.

and the inhabitants had very little money, but no doubt most of them worked on the land for the Lord of the Manor, or as servants in his hall, and possibly much of their food was provided, and they would have to rely on the bounty of the lord and his lady for extras at Christmas, at harvest-time, or when they were ill.

It will be noticed that there are three villagers on the list named "Feltwell". These Feltwells were probably descended from William Feltwell, "of Culforde", who in 1464 bequeathed by will (which may be seen in the Record Office of Bury St Edmunds) six ewes to Culford Church; he also left four ewes to Downham (probably Santon Downham), six ewes to his mother, and six ewes to his brother, John Feltwell. It would seem that William Feltwell was a sheep-farmer, or at least owned a flock in his own right. Maybe the "movables" belonging to Thomas Feltwell in the Subsidy List of 1524 were also sheep. It is interesting to notice that in his will William Feltwell mentions his wife, "Katarin" by name; a hundred years later a Catharin Feltwell was born at Culford, and the entry of her baptism may be seen in the Parish Register for 1562, and that of her twin brothers John and Thomas who were baptised a year previously, "on the 18 daie of June".

These were the children of Richard Feltwell, undoubtedly the same "Rychard Feltwelle" who was listed as earning a mere £1 per year in 1524. Now he was much more prosperous, since in a further Subsidy Return of 1568 he is taxed on "£5 in movables". He died in 1573 and was buried the "12 daie of Februarie". There is a further entry in the Register, of a Richard Feltwell and Ellen Lopham, who were "married on the 4th daie of Februarie, 1573", he may well have been a son of the older Richard, but the Feltwell family all visited Culford Church twice in February of that year, the first time for a wedding, and a week later for the funeral of Richard Feltwell. After his death there is no further mention of the Feltwells in the Parish Register, either their line died out or they left the village to seek fresh fields.

Throughout the years when the family of Feltwell lived in the village of Culford, typical of many such country folk, owning perhaps a few sheep or an ox, but serving all the time the Manor House, the Cootes held sway as Lords of the Manor.

Culford is often described by those who have never lived there as a "backwater"; and it is true to say that at the time of writing one of the chief characteristics of the place is an atmosphere of peace and seclusion, almost of escape from the cares around.

Judging by the scarcity of historical facts connected with Culford and the difficulty of tracing such information, it would seem that it has always been so; and yet to many people, throughout its story, possibly because of this very quality, it has always seemed a most desirable place in which to live.

Now the family of Coote came from Blo Norton in Norfolk, but there are no memorials to them there, nor are there any at Culford, excepting for their arms, which are incorporated in the West Window; but in the sixteenth century a certain Francis Coote, whose name appears on the Rolls of Cambridge University, became a Gentleman Usher to Queen Elizabeth I. When he died, in 1589, he was buried at South Lopham, Norfolk; this parish is very close to Blo Norton, and possibly was also a possession of the Cootes, and may well have been their final resting place.

Their connections with Culford are to be found in the State Papers, and from these we find that in the time of Henry VI a certain John Coote did homage to the Abbot of St Edmundsbury for his lands at Culford in 1435. Part of Culford used to be called Easthall, or Esthall, or Syffrewast Manor, after a certain Richard Syffrewast, who held it in fee of the Abbot in 1321. But in 1429 this land was transferred to John Coote "of Culforde", who thus paid homage for his joint possessions here. He was succeeded by his son, Richard, whose son and heir Richard, succeeded him, and this Richard was the father of Christopher Coote, who was Lord of the Manor of Culford in 1524, when Wolsey on behalf of the King levied his tax on the people in order to wage war against the King of France.

Nearly twenty years later came the Dissolution of the Monasteries, and after the spoliation of the Abbey by the King's Commissioners, the stripping of lead from its roof, the destruction of its bells and the pillaging of its sacred stones by the townsmen of St Edmundsbury — sights which many a Culford villager must have seen — the many possessions of manors and land belonging to the Monastery were granted by the King to various members of the nobility.

It seemed the natural thing that the Crown should grant the manor of Culford to Christopher Coote, whose family had lived here from 1429, possibly earlier. This grant may be seen in the State Papers:—

Granted in February, 1541.

Chr. Coote of Bloonorton, Norfolk, and Elizabeth his wife. Grant of the manor, and advowson of the Rectory of Culford, Suffolk, belonging to the late monastery of Bury St Edmunds with a portion of tithes in Culford, and a yearly pension of 8s. from the rectory; in as full manner as John Melford, alias Reve, late Abbot, held the same.

Westminster, 8 February, 32
Henry VIII.

There is, however, another entry in the State Papers, which states that in 1540 the Crown granted Culford, in Fee, for 488l. 15d. to Nicholas Bacon of London, who had licence to alienate or transfer the manor to his father, Robert Bacon.

This Nicholas Bacon was undoubtedly he who later became Sir Nicholas Bacon, Knight, Lord Keeper of the Great Seal; he was the second son of Robert Bacon of Drinkstone, Suffolk.

It will be seen that the grant to Nicholas Bacon was made only a year before the domain was granted to "Chr." Coote, and it would seem that the Cootes, being actually in possession of Culford until the Dissolution, pressed their claim to continue as Lords of the Manor despite the King's grant to Nicholas Bacon.

This they were successful in doing, since, when Christopher Coote died in 1563, the manor passed to his son and heir Richard, who died in 1580, being succeeded by his son and heir Nicholas.

Despite the troublesome nature of the mid-sixteenth century, one thing remained the same at Culford, the Cootes still reigned supreme as Lords of the Manor and the people were their servants. The Priests, indeed, first Joseph Balkey at the time of the Dissolution, and later Joseph Turnour in 1546, were more beholden to the Lord of the Manor than they had ever been; the "yearly pension of 8/-", now had to be paid to his Lordship instead of to the Abbot as in the old days, and their allegiance must now be first to the King and secondly to the family of Coote.

The year 1586, however, brought new changes and fresh faces to the village, and there must have been much speculation amongst the inhabitants as to how things would go in the future. It was forty-five years since Henry VIII had granted Culford to Christopher Coote, and during that time the Bacons of Redgrave, which was only two miles from Blowe, or Blo, Norton, the Cootes' original dwelling, never ceased to contest their claims to various manors and lands which had been granted to them by the Crown.

Culford, as has been stated, was one of these places; and after the death in 1579 of Sir Nicholas, the Lord Keeper, who had become a great favourite of Queen Elizabeth, his son, the new Sir Nicholas, made a determined effort to obtain this delightful place for himself and his family.

In 1586 Nicholas Coote gave way and Culford became the property of the Bacons. This is made abundantly clear in a document entitled "The Lord Keeper's account of all his landes", one of the Verulam Mss., transcribed some years ago by the Rev. L. Farrer, which contains the following:—

A deede of gift from Nicholas Coote of Blowe Norton (no longer "Bloo Norton") Co. Norfolk Esquier and Anne his wife to Sir Nicholas Bacon of Redgrave Co. Suffolk Knight and Anne his wife; of the whole manor of Culford and the manor of Easthall, or Esthall, in Culford, with all its messuages, etc. etc.

Dated 20th January, 28th year of Queen Elizabeth (Folio 157).

Also, amongst these same mss., "A remission, or release, from Nicholas Coote, Esquier of Blowe Norton and his heirs of all actions personal and quarrels, which he and his heirs may have against Sir N. Bacon, and his heirs. . . . ."

6th day of July, 28th of Queen
Elizabeth. (Folio 161).

It is interesting to notice that a certain Edmund Coote, B.A., of Peterhouse, Cambridge, was Headmaster of the Grammar School in Bury St Edmunds from 1596-97. He was the author of the *English Schoolmaster* which ran to forty editions. In spite of considerable research it has not been possible to prove that he was a descendant of the Cootes of Culford.

Nicholas Coote, therefore, and his wife Anne departed from Culford. He may have been the same Nicholas who was a pensioner of Trinity College, Cambridge, and knighted in 1603; if so, he went to live in Essex, but of this we cannot be sure.

The Parish Register, begun in 1560, when Robert Allen was Minister, records no marriages or burials at all in this eventful year of 1586; the Rector at the time, William Browne, entered only the baptisms of five babies, amongst them his own daughter Hester, "the 19th daie of Julie 1586". The next year, 1587, no less than twenty-two deaths are recorded, a large number for such a small community. There were indeed many changes.

Old friends had died, or had left with their old master, Nicholas Coote "Esquier", and there was a new Squire coming to live at Culford. It was said that he was to build a new magnificent hall, and that he had a large family, mostly sons. With such a large family at the Manor House, there would be work in plenty for local people, more money to spend when the pedlar called and more to take to Bury Fair, since it was rumoured that the new Squire was a rich man. Perhaps life under the Bacons' rule would be better. Who could tell?

3   The Bacons of Culford

THE sheep-reeve at the Monastery of Bury St Edmunds at the beginning of the sixteenth century was a certain Robert Bacon of Drinkstone, who came of good yeoman stock. His second son was Nicholas, later Sir Nicholas, and it is thought that he may have been educated at the school attached to the Monastery in Bury, but of this there is no proof. He later entered Corpus Christi College, Cambridge, and afterwards went to London, where he was called to the Bar in 1533. He soon seems to have made a reputation for himself, as being reliable, honest and courteous, and he quickly acquired Royal favour. Robert Reyce, a writer of the early seventeenth century, describes him as, "A man of such deep witt and experience in all matters of state and policye that in Forreyne countrees he was reputed of great fame and admiration, and at his death was accounted one of the greatest statesmen for wise counsell and deep policye that these parts of Christendom afforded". At the Dissolution of the Monasteries he received large grants of Abbey lands, including Redgrave and Botesdale. Redgrave became his country home, and Queen Elizabeth visited him and stayed at his mansion there. She often teased him about his over-fat form and once remarked in his hearing "Sir Nicholas's soul is lodged well". It was Queen Elizabeth who conferred on him the honour of knighthood and in 1558 made him the Lord Keeper of the Great Seal of England. In 1561 he was granted the Hundred of Blackbourne, one of the many former possessions of the Abbey of St Edmunds, with its sixty-four manors but, as we have seen earlier, Culford, one of the manors in this Hundred, was not transferred to him.

Sir Nicholas died in 1579 and it was not until 1586 that his son and heir, also Sir Nicholas, obtained Culford. This Sir Nicholas was the eldest son of the Lord Keeper by his first wife Jane, the daughter of William Fernley of West Creeting. The Lord Keeper's second wife was Anne, the daughter of Sir Anthony Cooke of Giddy Hall, Essex. She was a learned and pious woman, and the mother of Sir Francis Bacon, the Lord Chancellor; Sir Nicholas and Sir Francis were thus half-brothers. Nicholas was born in 1540, and when he was twenty-four he married Anne, a young girl of sixteen, the only daughter of Edmund Butts of Thornage, Norfolk.

Sir Nicholas and his Lady Anne had a large family of nine sons and three daughters. Queen Elizabeth made him a knight when she visited Norwich in 1578, and in later years he was the first person ever to be created a Baronet, when James I introduced the order in 1611. On the death of his father in 1579, Sir Nicholas inherited all the Lord Keeper's numerous lands and became a wealthy man in terms of real estate. Eventually he obtained also Culford from his near neighbour at Blowe Norton, Nicholas Coote, Esq., and in 1591 he built a mansion there. The old Manor House must have been fairly close to the Church, but Sir Nicholas decided to build on a mound to the west of the Church. The Hall was built of red brick, set square on the slight plateau of land, facing south, the same position, in fact, as the present building now occupies. Many years later, the French traveller and writer, de la Rochefoucauld, in 1784 described Culford Hall as "just like a great lantern, each of the four sides are so like any other that the first time we went there we did not know by which side we should enter. The number of windows is immense. The castle was built in Elizabeth's reign, very much in the Gothic style." Evidently, de la Rochefoucauld was not impressed, and when one looks at a print of the building it must be admitted that there is some truth in his opinion. Possibly it was considered quite the latest thing when it was built, and possibly, too, Sir Nicholas and his Lady Anne wished to have many windows so that they might look over their beautiful land from every corner of the house.

The Bacons often came to live at Culford, and what a hive of activity the Hall must have been. We mentioned that Lady Anne was the mother of twelve children, many of whom were grown-up by the time Culford Hall was built; their nearest neighbours were the Croftes of West Stow, with the family of Sir Thomas Kytson at Hengrave not far off. At Hawstead, beyond Bury St Edmunds and about six miles from Culford, lived Sir Robert Drury, one of the well-known family who gave their name to Drury Lane. Sir Robert's family were friendly with Sir Nicholas and Lady Anne, and in January of 1591 Anne Bacon, the eldest of the three daughters, was married to Sir Robert, she being nineteen and he seventeen. The young husband was a soldier with very little money until he attained his majority, and Sir Nicholas supported the young couple in quite a handsome fashion for the first few years, providing them with four menservants, two maidservants and four horses, in addition to the dowry of £1,600 he had given with his daughter. Young Lady Drury's first child was a girl whom she named Dorothy. The child was christened at Culford, as the entry in the Parish Register reads; "Dorothy Drury daughter of Sir Robert Drury Knight was baptised the 6 daie of June, 1593". Like so many other children of her time, the poor little girl did not live long, and in the chancel of Hawstead Church is a slab bearing the inscription:

> She, little, promis'd much;
> Too soone untyed:
> She only dreamt she liv'd,
> And then she dyde.

She was buried on 12th October, 1597, aged four years.

Unfortunately, relations between Sir Nicholas and his son-in-law deteriorated. Lady Drury spent much of her married life living at Culford under her father's roof, as her husband was away from home so much, but her father seemed to tire of her presence, or resented keeping her, and in the end Sir Nicholas brought an action against his son-in-law for "Recompence for my Ladie's Boarde, and for her children and servants for Vj yeares".

Sir Nicholas was probably not a very easy father-in-law; he spent a good deal of his time pressing claims of one sort and another, and was an exacting man. Nevertheless, he was known to be wealthy, and in those days of dowries and marriage settlements money counted for a great deal in the weddings of the landed gentry. Dorothy, the second daughter, was married at Culford on the 30th April, 1595 to Mr Bassingbourne Gaudie of Norfolk. Two years later her sister Gemimah on the 11th May 1597 married Sir William Waldegrave of Smallbridge, Suffolk.

Gervase Markham in *The English Housewife* (c.1600) says that for a wedding feast "about sixteen dishes were considered a suitable supply for the first course — possibly a shield of brawn, capon, boiled beef, chine of beef, neat's tongue, roast pig, minced chickens, roast goose, roast swan, turkey, venison, olive pie . . . . The housewife added as many salads and *quelque choses* as made 32 dishes which were considered as many as it was polite to put on the table for the first course. Then followed the second and third courses."

Was it possible to dance and sing after such a meal? We think it was: fair ladies had not such dainty appetites as those of today, and the gentlemen unashamedly relished their food, and undoubtedly danced with their ladies till nightfall.

It is not difficult to imagine with what pride and pleasure Sir Nicholas and Lady Anne showed Culford Hall to the wedding-guests; this new home, built on the land they had long coveted, theirs at last, with its many windows looking out over such beautiful quiet country. Standing on the terrace at the South front of the house, one could see parkland stretching away down to a small stream, and beyond that was the Heathland, the fringe of the Breckland, where the men and their ladies, too, could ride or hunt with the hawk, or course the hare with their hounds.

Probably Sir Nicholas had visions, as he showed his wedding guests around, of the lake he would make at Culford, by widening the stream where it flowed into the village below the Church. He had planted young oak and beech trees in the parkland, indeed there is an ancient oak in the park today, enclosed by iron palings, which is said to be the first oak planted by the Bacons; it is called "The King of the Park."*

Perhaps the ancient plane tree which still stands at the west of the lawn was also planted by him, as his step-brother, Sir Francis Bacon, is supposed to have introduced the plane tree into England, and it is very likely that this magnificent tree, with its wide-spreading branches, was given to Sir Nicholas by his brother. The plane trees at Hawstead near Bury St Edmunds are considered to be amongst the oldest in England, and it has always been supposed that these were given to Sir Robert Drury by his friend, Sir Francis Bacon.

Those Elizabethan days at Culford were probably some of the most colourful in its history, and there must have been great activity in the place and plenty of work for the villagers in caring for their Lord and his numerous family. One of the sons, Mr Butts Bacon, was married to Mistress Dorothie Jermyn in July 1611, and the following year his wife bore him a daughter, who was christened Anne; but the "Mistress Dorothie Bacon", who had married Mr Bassingbourne Gaudie, had a son, Anthonie, who was buried on 15th June 1606; and a "Mr John Bacon" was buried on

---

*I am indebted to the late gardener, Mr. James Skelton, for this information.

the "13th day of Januarie, 1605". He must have been one of Lady Anne's grandsons. Sorrow came as well as pleasure, even in their new surroundings.

Sorrow came also to others in the village, less fortunate than the Lord of the Manor and his family. Colourful days indeed were the days of the first Elizabeth, but they were cruel days as well, and there is one entry in the Parish Register which is the darkest blot on the page of the history of this quiet place:

A Register of such as have beene founde vagrant in the parish of Culford contrarie to the Statute in that case enacted.

Henrie Griffin, Ursula Griffin and Marie Griffin three fatherless children confessinge their parentes dwellings to have been in Dounam Market in Norfolke and that they were ther borne they were whipped and had their passporte made them the 28 daie of Februarie 1599.

A dark blot indeed.

The seventh son of the family was called Nathaniel; he had been six years old when his father built Culford House, and had grown to love it dearly. He was very quiet, scholarly and artistic, and perhaps because of his undoubted gifts he was the apple of his mother's eye, the Benjamin of the family, who remained a bachelor until he was twenty-eight, when he began to show an interest in the young and attractive widow of Sir William Cornwallis of Brome, near Eye.

4   Lady Jane

JANE Meautys was born, it is thought, in about 1581. She was the daughter of Hercules Meautys and his wife Philippe, daughter of Richard Cooke, of Gidea Hall, Essex. Jane's great-great-grandfather was a certain John Meautys, who came from Normandy with Henry VII as his secretary of the French tongue, and is supposed to have lived "at Greengate, by Leadenhall". His grandson was Sir Peter Meautys, the Ambassador to France, who obtained a grant of the manor of West Ham, in Essex. Sir Peter's son, Hercules, inherited the manor, and we suppose that Jane was born there.

Very little is known about her, until she became, in 1608, the second wife of Sir William Cornwallis, of Brome, in Suffolk.

Sir William came of a distinguished family. The family of Cornwallys or Cornwaleys was of some importance in Ireland in mediaeval times. A young son of the family, Thomas, went to live in London, and was a Sheriff of the City in 1378. He bought considerable estates in Suffolk, and his son John married the heiress of Ling Hall, one of the manors of Brome, near Eye. Subsequently, the two manors became one, and Brome Hall was the residence of the Cornwallis family from the sixteenth century, though they still lived at Ling Hall in 1506 when John Cornwallis, the great-grandson of the first John died. In his will he "bequeathed to the abbote of Bury myn ambulling nagge that I bought of John Revet". He was succeeded by his brother Edward, who was succeeded by his brother Robert, who was succeeded by his brother William. This William became the great-grandfather of the Sir William who married Jane Meautys or Mewtas, who mentioned him in her will and arranged for a tomb-stone to be placed in Oakley Parish Church, where he was buried. His son was Sir John who distinguished himself in the Navy and was knighted for his bravery and was also made steward of the household of Prince Edward. There is an ornate tomb to his memory in the Church at Brome.

He was succeeded by his son Thomas, who was knighted on the 1st December 1548. He was a notable member of the family, being made Sheriff of Norfolk and Suffolk in 1553, and in 1557 Comptroller of Queen Mary's Household. He was in high favour with Mary, and enjoyed her confidence, but he lost his political importance, and his offices, when Elizabeth I ascended the throne. He then retired to the country, where he rebuilt his house in Brome, and lived in comfort until his death on the 26th December, 1604, aged eighty-six. He was buried in Brome Church, where there is a fine tomb erected to his memory, with the following inscription:

> Here lies Sir Thomas Cornwallis, son of Sir John, who was of Queen Mary princely councell, and Treasurer of Cales, and after comptroller of her Majestie's household, in especial grace and trust of his mistress at her untimely death.

It was his son, Sir William, who became the husband of Jane Meautys. He appears to have been a very able man; at the age of eleven he was entered as a student at Trinity College, Cambridge and in 1599 was knighted in Dublin for his services in Ireland.

His first wife was the Lady Lucy, one of the daughters of Lord Latimer, and the mother of two sons, William, who died young, and Thomas, and four daughters, Frances, Elizabeth, Catherine and Dorothy.

When Jane Meautys became, at the age of twenty-seven, the second wife of Sir William, she found herself the step-mother of five grown-up children, and it is small wonder that when she gave birth two years later to a son, Frederick, she lavished on him intense affection and always jealously guarded his rights.

Little Frederick, born in November, 1610, was only a year old when his father, Sir William died, and his mother, now Jane, Lady Cornwallis, became his legal guardian. Sir William had left a great part of his estate to his elder son, Thomas, the child of his first wife, but he bequeathed to his second wife the manors of Brome, Oakley, Stuston, Thrandeston, Palgrave, and the manor of Wilton in Yorkshire.

Frederick's mother devoted herself to his upbringing, having him educated at home under her care. She was a somewhat serious-minded young woman, completely satisfied with her life as the Lady of the Manor, a position which she admirably fulfilled. She had one close friend at Court, Lucy, Countess of Bedford, a vivacious woman who remained a faithful friend to Lady Jane as long as she lived. She was a Woman of the Bedchamber to Anne of Denmark, the wife of James I, and was acknowledged one of the beauties of her day. Lady Bedford and Lady Cornwallis corresponded regularly, and many of the letters of the Countess Lucy to Lady Jane have been preserved. Although she spent a great part of her time in Court circles, and kept Lady Jane well-informed of all that was going on, the Countess of Bedford nevertheless had a great love of gardens, and when she retired to Moor Park in Hertfordshire she laid out a very beautiful garden, and we find her writing to Jane on 4th October, 1618. "This monthe putts me in minde to intreate the performance of youre promise for some of the little white single rose rootes, I saw at Brome, and to chalenge Mr Bacon's promise for some flowers, if about you ther be any extraordinary ones, for I am now very busy furnishing my gardens".

The "Mr Bacon" mentioned in Lady Lucy's letter was none other than Nathaniel Bacon of Culford Hall, who in 1613 began to be interested in Lady Cornwallis. Elizabeth, the sister of her former husband, Sir William Cornwallis, had married Sir Thomas Kytson of Hengrave Hall about two miles distant from Culford, and what more natural than that Jane should visit her sister-in-law, and that Mr Bacon should have ridden over from Culford to visit his father's neighbour? However it was, he began to pay court to her, at first through the good offices of the Rev. Elnathan Parr, D.D., the Rector of Palgrave, Suffolk, a friend of the Bacons of Redgrave and of the Cornwallis family, in whose benefice was Palgrave. The first hint of Nathaniel Bacon's interest in Lady Cornwallis is found in a letter of her Ladyship to Mr Parr:

Jane Lady Cornwaleys to Mr Parr.

Mr Parr, — I hope you do so well remember what I said to you, at your being here, as that you have not given no incoregement to the gentleman to prosede in that matter, for, as I tould you then, I saye now, that since Sir Willem Cornwaleys's death I neaver as yet had a thought of changing the course of life which I now lede. What may be my fortune hereafter I know not, for it is onli known to Him which is the disposer of all things; whom I beseche so to direct me in all my courses as may be most to his glori: but this gentleman being so desirous to see me, as you said he was, I thought then and so I do now, it ware uncivell part of me to forbid him coming, but left it, you know, to himselfe, and so I do still.

Yor asseured frend,
JA. Cornwaleys

(1614)
To my kind frend, Mr Parr at Palgrave.

Theirs was not an easy courtship, and "my kind frend, Mr Parr", must have had a somewhat trying time in acting as go-between. There was great concern about land and property on both sides; Sir Nicholas and Lady Bacon, Nathaniel's parents, were loth to give Culford Hall as a marriage-portion to their son, favourite though he seemed to be; and Lady Jane, though inheriting several estates from her late husband, nevertheless coveted Culford for the sake of young Frederick. There was a lengthy correspondence before agreement was reached, as will be seen by the following extracts: Mother of Nathaniel, Anne Lady Bacon, to Mr Parr.

We have offered what we are abell, and what we can and will faythfully performe. If it be accepted, we shall rejoyce much therein; if not, we must be contented without grudging, asseuring ourselves it is the Lord's doing. And although the jewell layd before us be never so riche, if we be not abill to buy it we must be content to forbeare it. We must not laye out all our stock upon one purchas, having so many others to provide for.

To which Jane, Lady Cornwallis, indignantly replied:

Mr Parr . . . . and wareas you saye that Sir Nicholas and my La, expects their son should have soch grate prefarment by me, I must answer againe, that they have made it seeme other wayes to me, in asseuring me that it was myselfe, and not my fortune, which they desiered; but I confess, by several circumstances I maye justly feare that I shall find my fortune to be the chief motive which hath persuaded them to this; besides which, if I do, yet it will much discourage me for persevering any furder in it. . . .

J. C.

(1613)   (and also)

Mr Parr . . . . I must tell you that I did never expect that you would have been a persuader of me, to agave away the increase of my owne estate, being you have eaver heard me earnestli to protest that I would not, though I had married to a much greater fortune then Sir N Bacon doth offer with his son: for I would never have done my child so much wronge, though I might have had all the good of the world by it.

1613.

Feeling seemed to be running high, but evidently Nathaniel still pursued his courtship, and wrote to Lady Cornwallis from Culford on 6th March, 1614.

Sweet Madam,

The unwished for newes in oe contrye maketh me desier the entertaynement of my speciale consolements wth you for the vntymelye death of the Lord Harrington, and leaueth me so sensible of oue frayle estate in this lyfe that I cannot but wth my gratest oratory solycite a better assurance for the enioyinge of yoe sweetest companye. Deare Madam, make me happy in my chiefest desiers by yoe speedy retourne, wch is equally enuited by other conueniences. My father and mother ar determyned to make a longe journeye to Maubourne hilles presently after the feast of oe Lady, before wch tyme I thincke yoe presence is necessarily required. Remember yoe promise in cominge downe by my fathers, wch seemeth specially conuenient unto me. The hast of the messenger biddeth me kyss yoe hands, wishinge you all happyness and restinge entyerly yours,

Nath. Bacon.

Culford, March 6th (1614).

For my Lady Bedford, let my best seruise attend her, and my continual prayers for all comfort, spiritual and temporal.

To the most honoured Lady, the Lady Jane Cornewalleys, at Mrs Cooke's* house by Charing Cross, geue these.

In the end peace was restored and Nathaniel's mother wrote to her future daughter-in-law.

---

*Presumably Lady Jane's mother.

Madam,

Yor delaye in cominge downe hath caused you once againe to be trobled with my deer Nath at London. I am sorry that your busynes doth carye you another way and that I shall not see you at Culford in your jorney towards Broome. But it shall not be longe I trust in God before I see you in a neerer affinity then yett ever I did, in which I joye muche now; and I doubt not but you shall muche more joye in it, when I am with the Lord God in Heaven. My husband commends him very kindly unto you, and we bothe doe very willingly give unto you the juill of our deer sonne. God blesse you together with abbundance of all felicity in this lyfe, and in the lyfe to come the presence of the Blessed Trinity, a greater happiness cannot be to any. Deer La. the blessed God be with you for ever.

Yors
Anne Bacon.

(1614)

To my most deerly beloved the Lady Jane Cornwallis give this, at London.

So it was that on the 1st of May, 1614, Jane Lady Cornwallis, and Mr Nathaniel Bacon were married in Brome Parish Church, and they lived very happily together till death divided them. Nathaniel was four years younger than his wife, a quiet studious man, very fond of botany and a gifted artist. Those of his paintings which have survived are now in the possession of Lord Verulam; there is a postscript to one of his letters to his wife, 19th May, 1624, when she was staying in London with the Countess of Bedford, which refers to his painting:

Mr Parr, Mrs Parr, and Mr Greenhill remember their best servis. My service to all my friends, and bid John Fenn to send my coullers as soon as possible.

Mr Nathaniel Bacon and his "Sweet Hart", as he so often addressed her in his letters when she was away from home, lived at first at Brome Hall, only paying occasional visits to Culford. Their first child, a girl, named Anne after Nathaniel's mother, was born in 1615, and a boy, Nicholas, in 1617. We may be sure that these children lived a happy life in the peaceful Brome Hall, with its gardens and roses, with their kindly, careful mother, and their studious father. Their quiet country life was often relieved by a visit from their mother's cousin, Sir Thomas Meautys, who was devoted to her and her family, or from the Countess of Bedford, who must have brought many tales of life at court to pass the long evenings. Sometimes she persuaded Lady Jane to pay a return visit to London, but not always; on one occasion when Lady Jane should have been in London, Nathaniel fell ill, and the Lady Lucy wrote to her friend as follows:

Dear Cornewallis,

I send this bearer to inquire of my sicke freinds, into which number I am extream sorry to hear Mr Bacon is fallen, both for his own sake and yours, and as desirous as any can be to hear of his amendment, which I hartely pray for, and hope to reseave the good news of att this messenger's retorne. I heard not of his being ill till my Lo. Chamberlain told me of itt, and that upon that occasion you had excused your selfe from coming to the Queen's funeral, whear I hoped to have seen you, and am doubly sorry upon this occasion to faile of that contentment; ear long I trust a happier one will bring us with gladnes to meete, which I wish to you in as great a measure as I do to

Your most affectionat freind and servant,
L. Bedford.

The K. is earnest to have the funeral hastened and sayeth itt shall be on Saturday* com se'night; but, for all that, I thinke itt will not be till this day fortnight.

Bedford, in haste, this Thursday morning.
(April 1619)

Shortly before the Queen's death, King James visited Sir Nicholas Bacon at Culford, taking with him Prince Charles, later Charles I. They were staying at Newmarket and went to Sir Nicholas Bacon's to dinner "to see a young gentlewoman, daughter to Sir Bassingbourne Gaudy that is dead long since." The young gentlewoman's mother was the Mistress Dorothy Bacon who had married Mr Gaudie at Culford in April 1595, and they were evidently staying with her father, Sir Nicholas. It is recorded that the King, the Prince, and the Lord of Buckingham were greatly impressed by Mistress Anne, and she was "much made of by them all"; Prince Charles was so overcome that he wrote verses in her honour.

---

*The funeral took place on 13th May.

Nevertheless, Jane was not always a stay-at-home, and Nathaniel sometimes looked after the children, either at Brome, or at their grandfather's house at Culford. Their grandmother, Lady Anne Bacon, had died when they were very small, and it was company for the old Sir Nicholas to have his "dear Nath", and his grandchildren to stay; Nathaniel was useful in the management of the estate, and it was very pleasant to watch small figures running across the lawns of Culford Hall. Nathaniel wrote to his wife on one such occasion:

Sweet Hart,

I receiued yoe letter, wherby I understand of the slow proceeding of oe business, and for myne owne part her, I cannot be so well pleased but I much desier dayly to be wth you, wherfore I desier you to send me word by the next whether my cominge may be inconuenient or not, and how longe you meane to stay. For my cominge, I cannot wright any things certayne; for my horses ar infected wth other sick horses and so extreamely sick that I know not whether they will liue or not. For my health, I cannot wright as I did last; for this week I suffered more payne in my teeth then euer, and this night I slept not one hower, and am now goinge to the mountebanck at Bury to draw them out. For ye children, they ar in very good health. Nick sends you word of a brood of young chickens, and of a disaster he escaped at my beinge with him, for he eate so much milk porrage at supper that he cryed out, (O Lord!) I think I haue almost broake myne gutt; and I was fayne to walk him a turne or ij about the chamber to digest yt.

Newes I cann wright none; wherfore I desier you onely to entertayne my earnest desiers to enjoy youe company, then wch nothing can be more pleasing to him who is and shall be allwaies onely.

Yours,

(1624)   Nath. Bacon.

To his moste noble friend the Lady Jane Cornewalleys, at Harington Howse, geue these.

Nicholas seems to have had the same hearty appetite as any other boy, and tooth-ache was as painful three hundred years ago as it is today, but none of us need suffer the tender ministrations of a "mountebanck" to cure it. But the next letter dated the 15th May, 1624, brings the Culford of those days very close to ourselves for it speaks of the lake:

Sweet Hart,

I haue now receiued yoe letters wth much satisfaction to my desiers by vnderstandinge of yoe health, and safe arriuall at London after so troublesome journey, and do retourne vnto the healthfull estate of oe children and my self, who haue since yoe departure (thanks be to God) suffered very little in my brest. I do wonder much that the commission was not retourned in the prescribed tyme, since I my self beinge at Norwich with Mr Morse did so much vrge yt to Mr Sherwood, who promised to retourne yt wth out fayle; nethyer haue I hearde any thinge of yt since yoe departure, being not able to comend any thing concerninge that business but my many wishes for yoe frutefull endeauors in the proceeding.* My father her hath taken me so wholy vpp to his seruise, hauinge at this tyme 50 men at worke in castinge his great pond, that I can hardly tyme to look home, being my selfe also studious to obserue him with my best wits for the better effecting of myne and yoe desiers. You shall receiue by this bearer yoe wastecote, hauinge receiued yt this day from Brome wth the health of oe children. I could gladly vnderstande some tyme for the expectation of yoe retourne, but I do expect uncertayntye in vt from vncertaynety of oe business; being assured that wth its licence our mutuall loues shall receiue quickly ther mutuall desiers in each other's presence. In the meane tyme, I leaue yt, with my selfe, wholely to yoe disposing; and youe self attended wth the best prayers of him who wilbe alwaies,

Yoe

Nath. Bacon.

I pray speak to John Fenn to buy me 3 ownces of masticott more than I wrote for, and it need not be of the best sort, yt being for yoe seate, wch was sett vpp the last Satterday. We haue payed a subsidie and halfe to the beneuolence. My seruice to all wth you.

Culford, May 15th (1624).

---

*It seems likely that Lady Jane was helping to set the wheels in motion towards Nathaniel Bacon being made a knight.

To his most worthy friend the Lady Cornwalleys, at the Lady Cooke's howse by Charing Cross, geue these.

This "great pond" was the beginning of the lake as we know it, and stayed as Sir Nicholas first made it, in 1624, until 1791 when it was enlarged by J. H. Repton. The stream which ran through Culford, to the south of the Church, in the seventeenth century, is the same stream which had given the village its name; it is a very small stream, canalised now in the nature of a drainage ditch, and still flows into the lake at Culford near the church, leaving it to enter the River Lark at West Stow at the far end of the lake.

The making of his "great pond" was one of the last tasks undertaken by Sir Nicholas, for he died the same year and was buried at Redgrave, under the altar tomb he had had made in the church for his wife the Lady Anne and himself, and his sons paid the sculptor Nicholas Stone the sum of £200 to carve the figures of Sir Nicholas and his Lady in white marble lying full length on top of the tomb, where they may be seen to this day.

> The Body of Nicholas Bacon Knight and
> Baronet lieth here: He took to Wyfe Anne
> Butts sole Heyre to Butts and Halfe Heyre to Bures
> They lived together 52 yeares, when Death makinge
> The separation on Hir Part, He Erected This
> Monument to Them Both. Ano Domini 1616
> The Lady
> Ann Bacon Wife of the same Nicholas Bacon
> Lyeth buryed in this place, by whom he had
> 9 sonnes and 3 daughters, she dyed in the 68
> year of her age, the 19 day of September
> Ano Domini 1616

After the death of his father, Culford became Nathaniel's property, together with the sum of one thousand pounds per year for its upkeep, and he writes, "I have cast upp superficially the inventory of all the stock and movables of Culford, with the legacies to be payed out, the plate excepted, and yt amounteth to 1200,40 and odd pounds. My brother Coleby hath offered to buy the stock of kyne and horses and to hyre so much ground as now resteth in mine owne hands, but I have differed my resolution."

One supposes that Lady Jane was gratified that her husband had "differed his resolution", since she was anxious to keep the estate in her own family. Although Brome Hall was still kept up as a residence, the Bacon family lived from that time almost exclusively at Culford. And in 1625 Mr Nathaniel Bacon was drawn out of his serenely quiet life in the country, and called to London, where he was created a Knight of the Bath in honour of the Coronation of Charles I; thus Jane, Lady Cornwallis, became Lady Jane Bacon, Lady of the Manor of Culford, and she walked in the coronation procession with her husband, Sir Nathaniel. That she was attractive we know, slim and erect, with fair hair, pink and white complexion and shapely hands, and we believe she was a good Lady of the Manor. Her will shows how carefully she looked after the estate, and her correspondence proves how kind and considerate she was to her many impecunious relatives. Her own and Nathaniel's family now consisted of two girls and a boy, since a third child, Jane, was born in 1624, and there was, of course, young Frederick, her former husband's child, now a boy of about sixteen.

But the busy, peaceful life of Lady of Culford could not last unsullied for ever. Sir Nathaniel was not a strong man, in many of his letters to his wife he speaks of his poor health, and by 1627 he was becoming weaker. A letter from Sir Thomas Meautys, Lady Jane's cousin, is the first news of Nathaniel's illness:

My ever best Lady and Cousin,

I have, almost ever since my coming from Culford, been dayly in journeys, and am, at the writing of thease, soe newly alighted from my horse, that I have scarse time, considering the carrier's hower is at hand, to scribble this. I am not a little compatible with my friends thear to find, by a letter from my cousin Fred, that my cousin Bacon's health still declines, and that your Lapp hath hurt your foot, which puts you to much payne. Madam, weare I good for any thing that mought bee of use towards eyther of your recoveries, I would not fayle to hasten to you, and make a tender in person of my best endeavours and most affectionat service; but since I am not, my onely resort must bee with my dayly prayers, upon the knees of my heart, to the Great Physician Himself. Nevertheless, I have hearwithall sent some of that syropp of ela campane, of my sister's making, which I have myself, and some other of my friends, found so much good of, and have withall sent the receipt herinclosed by which it is made; and if thear bee any thing in it hurtful to my cosin's informity, yett I am perswaded it will do your Lapp good for that rheume whearwith I heard you complayne your wear troubled a-mornings. And by cause I saw my cosin was allowed to take tobacco somtimes, I, having had some sent mee from a friend for speciall good, have hearwithall likewise sent some porcion of it, and, yf my cosin like it, I will send him some more. Soe, wishing you all my soule a share in eyther of your sufferings and discomforts of body or mynd, so that your parts therby might be the more tolerable, I comend you to the consolacion and protection of God Almighty, and rest,

Yo^r LaPP'^{s} all and ever to love and serve you,

T. Meautys.

June 22 (1627)

The Duke, they say, sette sayle on Weddensday, and the King is expected hear tomorrow. Yt is no newes to you, I conceave, that Sir Thomas Meautys* is father of a brave boy, and that my Lady of Sussex hath in congratulacion thereof, descended from her greatness and is like to be well again with him.

Alas, the "syropp" was not able to do any good for the sick man, and in June he died at the age of forty-two, leaving his wife a widow for the second time. This year, 1627, was a particularly unhappy one for Lady Jane, she lost not only her dear Nathaniel, but her good friend the Countess of Bedford, and in October her little Jane, aged three years, passed away. What desolation must have filled the once-joyous Culford Hall, how melancholy seemed Sir Nicholas's lake, and how still the Church where Nathaniel and little Jane lay. For Sir Nathaniel and his little daughter were both buried in Culford Church, and the entries of their burials follow each other in the Parish register:

Sir Nathaniel Bacon Knight of the bath was buryed the first of July 1627.

Mris Jane Bacon daughter of Sir Nathaniel deceased was buryed the 31st of October.

Jane Bacon experienced intense sorrow; Culford, which she had coveted, was hers, but hers, too, were the lonely years of widowhood stretching ahead. But she had much to do, and many things to see to; she first erected a memorial to her husband's memory

---

*Lady Jane's brother.

which is now on the north wall of the porch of Culford Church, showing a bust of Sir Nathaniel, which, according to a letter written to Lady Jane by her brother-in-law, Sir Edmund Bacon, is a very good likeness; there is an artist's palette and brushes at each corner of the tablet reminding us of his skill as a painter.

Then she quietly continued with the business of living, of managing her numerous estates and farms, with the help of her agent, Mr Morse, and of bringing up her children. In addition to her own children she brought up her brother's child, Hercules, and, later, her son's children. Her brother, Sir Thomas Meautys, not to be confused with her cousin of the same name, was a soldier by profession and seemed quite unable to manage his affairs; almost every letter to his sister, even his letter commiserating with her on the loss of her husband, ended with a request for money. She settled an annuity on him and his equally poverty-stricken wife, and paid for the upbringing of their children, until a letter from a friend advised her that "it is high tyme the childe* were taken into some better keepinge, for the nurse doth her parte to the uttmost, yett he now begins to growe, and will look for better comons than her wages will beare. He thrives the better for his good Aunt Bacon's allowance, wch is weekely sent his nurse for him".

So young Hercules Meautys came to live at Culford under the care of his Aunt; he was said to be "slowe to learn, which came not from dullness of wit, but rather from wildness, which tyme might alter in him". So wrote his father to Lady Jane!

Thus Lady Jane Bacon, still a youngish woman of forty-six, found plenty to occupy her at Culford. We read of her sending "a dainty pott of jellye" to a lady friend, and the gift of a pike to Sir Edmund Bacon, her brother-in-law, who wrote to her "There are thankes to be given under my hande for the best and fattest pike that ever was eaten: he had a fish hooke in the fatt on ye out-side of his rivett". (Redgrave, Suffolk, 19 April, 1628).

She was indeed always thinking of the needs of someone, and her kindness was known to all. The Queen of Bohemia, sister to Charles I said of Lady Jane to her brother, Sir Thomas Meautys, "Your sister is one of the best dispositions in the world, and every way I doe love her very well, and better than any lady in England that I knowe, and have a great deale of reason to do soe".

---

*Hercules, the eldest boy.

After his meeting with the Queen, Sir Thomas wrote as follows to Lady Jane:

Deare Sister,

By this you shall receive an account of the present that you left with me for the Queen of Bohemia. As soone as she saw me come into the roome where Hir Matie was, her second words was, "How dooth my Lady Cornwallis"? I gave her your present, and told her that I had left you with a hart charged with griefe for the death of your husband, but with a minde full of will and reddyness to doe her majesty service. She tooke the box, and before all the company that was there did open it, and did very much commend the property of it, and retourne you many thanks; for that I saw that it was a gyft very agreeable to her, for the same day at my Lord Ambassador's howse, where the King and Queene and Princess of Orange, did dyne, she tooke occasion to speake of it againe, and said that the old love between you two must not be forgotten.

July 25th 1627.

5   Sir Frederick Cornwallis

FREDERICK Cornwallis was a young man of seventeen when his step-father, Sir Nathaniel Bacon, died. He appears to have been a likeable boy; he was described by a writer of his day as being "of an easy, thoughtless disposition, being of so resolved a mind that no fear came into his thoughts; well-spoken, and of a comely and goodly personage". His uncle, Sir Charles Cornwallis, of whom his mother was not very fond, took some interest in him, and was able to get young Frederick into the service of the Court. It is probable that he was one of the attendants who accompanied Charles I on his journey to Spain in search of a bride. Some writers have said that Frederick accompanied Prince Henry, Charles's elder brother, to Spain, but as Henry died in 1612, and Frederick was born in 1610, it is not very likely; but we do know that he served Charles I "from his youth with great fidelity", and it seems possible that it was Charles whom he waited upon. In May of the year that his step-father died, 1627, he was created a Baronet, by the influence of his mother's cousin, Sir Thomas Meautys, who was Clerk to the Council, and at the same time was made an Equerry to the King his young master, now Charles I.

Maybe because he was at court, where he would meet many charming ladies, and maybe, too, because she knew he had a great deal of charm, his mother, Lady Jane, about this time started to look around for a suitable wife for Sir Frederick. There is one rather amusing letter from her cousin, Mistress Dorothy Randolph, who was sent by Lady Jane to spy out the land and make judicious enquiries:—

> My most Honoured Lady,
>
> There was one question my Lady Barrington asked me when she was in towne that I would desire to be provided of answer from you for her against she come. She desired to know if Sir William Curteen asked what portion you would demand, what she should say. We looke for her every day; and my cosin Meautys's man put me in hope I should see you here between this and Easter, which was very welcome newes to

me. I have enquired after matches in other places if this should faile, but can hear of none but some of the nobility which I harkened not to, becaus I thinke you desire not to match with them; yet thear was one Lord whoes daughters weare so much comended to me, that I did not absolutely denie it, but thought good to let you know. It is my Lord of Bridgwater*; and Sir Henry St George if he propounded it, whoe is well acquainted with him, and he will give six thousand pounds. When you come I hope you will met with one to your liking, which I hope will be shortly; till which time, and ever, I am and will be

Your humble servant,

(1629).   Dorothe Randolph

But whilst Lady Jane and Mistress Randolph were busying themselves in trying to find a suitable wife for Sir Frederick, he had already met someone with whom he "desired to match". She was Mistress Elizabeth Ashburnham, one of the daughters of Sir John Ashburnham, a lady-in-waiting at the Court and a Maid of Honour to Henrietta Maria, Charles I's Queen. This young lady and Sir Frederick fell in love, without any question of allowances, or of what Sir John was willing to give as a "portion"; Charles and his Queen favoured the alliance, and encouraged the pair to marry, promising to settle £3,000 on them. And so they were married, the King and Queen were present and doubtless many friends of the bridal pair, but the bridegroom's mother was not even informed.

When Lady Jane discovered that her son, her beloved Frederick on whom she had spent so much time and thought, was married, without even consulting her, her indignation knew no bounds. A parent in these days would be very much hurt to be so treated, but three hundred years ago, when parents were held in much greater respect than they are today, the act was almost unforgivable; and being of so direct and forthright a nature, she sat down and wrote a stinging letter to her wayward son. To which he replied "I cannot but bee extremly troubbled at my one misfortune, in that it appears to you (and I confesse it may verie well appear so)

---

*John, Earl of Bridgwater, President of Wales, had issue by the Lady Frances Stanley, second daughter and co-heir of Ferdinand Earl of Derby, four sons and eleven daughters, of which he saw seven honourably married before his decease in 1649. They were the young persons for whom Milton wrote the Masque of Comus, on the occasion of one of them, Lady Alice Egerton, having been lost in Haywood Forest.

that I am the worst of children to the best of mothers . . . . . I beseach you doe not cast of and lose your childe, who neither can nor will bee happie without your LaPP's favor, and who with that regained will ever strive and I hope shall prove to bee as great a comfort as hiether two he hath proved otherwise; this is the onelie act which hath manifested mee to bee as you pleese to tearme it your unnaturall childe".

Lady Jane, however, was not so easily moved, and it was not until both the King and Queen had written to her on behalf of her son and his bride, that she relented and took them into her favour.

The King to Jane Lady Bacon.

Charles R.

Trustie and well beloved, we greete you well. In o^r gratious favo^r to a faithful and worthie servant to o^r dearest consort, wee were pleased to hono^r yor sonne's marriage both with o^r royall presence and by admittinge the ceremonie to be done in a place where none have accesse but such as the Kinge purposeth to hono^r. Hereby wee doubt not but (as you have just cause) you have receyved much comfort, and to increase it further, by removening all misprision, w^h by the shortnesse to tyme governed by o^r affaires might happen, wee hereby will you to attend us at Newmarket, whither we purpose speedilye to repaire, and where you shall understand o^r further pleasure and grace towards yor son.

Given at o^r court at Whitehall, the fourth day of January, in the sixth year of o^r reigne.

(1630-31) Sealed with the royal arms.

There followed the meeting at Newmarket, Lady Jane riding over, accompanied by her maid and probably Mr Morse and her younger son Nicholas. The young King, elegant and striking in his appearance, must surely have been moved by the sight of this slim, good-looking young widow who made her deep obeisance to him. And she, Lady Jane, how could she refuse the request of the King himself? In later years, when grim tragedy ended Charles's life, how often must she have pictured her meeting with him here at Newmarket, and his kindly concern for her son.

After her visit to Newmarket, Lady Jane received the following letter from the Queen:—

The Queen to Jane Lady Bacon

To o[r] Right Trustie and Right Well Beloved The Lady Bacon. Henriette Marie R.

Right trustie and right well beloved, we greet you well. Wee are so sensible of the respect that you have shewd to o[r] request, in receyving againe your sonne into yo[r] favor, that wee cannot chuse but let you know that wee take it very thankfully at your hands. If wee can prevaile but this much further with you, that you will extend the same kindness towards your daughter in law, and so receive them both into yo[r] motherly care, you shall put such an obligation upon us as wee shall never forget, but remember upon all occasions wherein our favour can be of any use unto you, and, with this assurance, wee committ you to the protection of the Almightie.

Given under o[r] hand at Newmarket, this one and thirty day of January (1630-31).

Who could resist such persuasive kindness? The quarrel was thus ended, and Lady Bacon was goodness itself once her annoyance was over, and proved herself a never-failing source of comfort to her daughter-in-law when the babies began to arrive. Sir Frederick and his young wife were mostly at court in attendance on the King and Queen, which was no life for infants, and there was Culford on whose green lawns Sir Frederick and his step-brother and sister had played, with the lake to fish in, and horses to ride; what better life could they have than to live with their grandmother? First came little Charles, baptised at Culford on the 19th April 1632, then Henrietta Maria, named after the Queen, and baptised at Culford on the 20th July 1634. Frederick was born in September 1636; and there was a fourth child, George. These children were brought up under their grandmother's careful eye along with Hercules Meautys, her nephew. They must have made a pretty picture as they ran about Culford Hall in their lovely, simple Stuart dresses, soft and elegant, so different from the stiff, stilted fashions of the Elizabethan children. Their Uncle Nicholas, grandmother's youngest son, was a student at Trinity College, Cambridge, who no doubt visited Culford in the vacations. The following copies of two of his letters to Lady Jane are interesting and amusing, and so different in style from the writings of a son to his mother in these days:

Deare Mother,

I might bee accused of a greate deal of negligence, if I shoulde not, as often as I have any occasion, present my most humble duty unto your laP; and I hope, Maddame, to perforem your LaP's promise to my tutor for mee in regaining ye time I have lost. Maddame, ye tailor saieth, for gownes, either a wrought silk gregorine or a tuffe taffety in graine, ye colour greene or tawny, which your LaP pleaseth; for sowing hee requireth fourteen yardes for ye gowne, besides the facings, of half a yarde broade.

N.B.

Cambridge, May 23 (1635).

Dear Mother,

I never faile as oft as occasions shew themselves of presenting my humble duty to your LaP. I doe count it a great happiness, that, whilst I am deprived of your LaP's sight, I have the opportunity to doe so in writing; and I very much wishe, Maddam, I could as well expresse it in words as it is really in my heart; but your LaP knoweth my dissability that way, and therefore I hope you will excuse all faults committed in the writing. Thus, Maddam, humbly craving your LaP's blessing, I rest, Maddam,

Yo^r LaP's most obedient childe,
Nic. Bacon.

My aunt Walgrave presents her humble service. Maddam, I shall desire yor LaP to buy mee a blacke hatt, for that bever I have begins to decay.

(1635)

To my deare and loving mother, the Lady Bacon, presente these.

Lady Jane's cousin, Sir Thomas Meautys, still continued to write to her, in most affectionate terms, and often came to Culford to see her and the children, and "my precious cousin Anne"; but season followed season, the young oaks shed their leaves in autumn, and the children helped to gather the acorns, the plane tree planted when Sir Nathaniel was young was growing taller, and Lady Jane would watch it coming into leaf each spring, always hoping that the children's father and mother would be coming soon, yet the children saw very little of their parents. Sir Frederick and Lady Elizabeth were busy in their life at court, very often in debt and finding it difficult at times to make ends meet. Sir Frederick was, like his mother's brother, hopeless at managing money matters, as his mother had come to know full well, and as these letters will show:

Extract from letter of Elizabeth, wife of Sir Frederick Cornwallis, to Lady Jane Bacon, the 4th February, 1635.

Madam, my husband is very good; but, if he put his estate into a stranger's hand, I shall never looke to see any part of it again: but for your favor to me in desiring to keep my joynture free, I cannot say enuff, but I shall laye it up in a thankful harte with yor many other kindnesses. But I hope my husband will be willing to give your Lap any assurance that you pleas, and trewly, Madam, the more tie you have upon him and his estate, the gladder I shall be, for I veryly believe it will be best for him and I pray God give us all a happie meeting.

Sir F. Cornwallis to his mother:— 26.11.1635.

. . . . for that wch I shall say to you of my selve will bee none, wch is, that I have in faine to pay away all the little monie that Mr Morse brought to stop some few people's mouths, and yet it will not halfe satisfie them; so that I have not a shilling left for my selve, nor know not what to doe, unless your LaP will bee pleased to take mee into your consideration, wch if your LaP shall please to doe now at this time, you will eternally oblige, madam,

Your Lap's most affectionately obedient sonne,
F. Cornwallis.

Thanks to Lady Jane the family was provided for, and Mr Morse was constantly taking sums of money to London to keep the wolf from Sir Frederick's door.

In 1639, Sir Frederick was elected to Parliament for the Borough of Eye, which might occasionally have brought him closer to Culford, but even so, the children's mother paid very infrequent visits to her mother-in-law, as is evident from the following letter:

Deare Mother,

I humbly thanke you for your kind letter and desire of my company, which truly Madam is very pleasinge to me, and I shude be very glad to see prattling Frede, yor LaP, and all the rest of my good friends at cheerly Culford, if I coulde: but, alas, Madam, I feare I shall not this sumere, because it is so

neer spent . . . . I beseeche yor La^p to bless them all . . . .
White-Hall, the 15 August, 1639.

By this time the political situation was becoming acute, and Sir Frederick, always loyal to the King, followed Charles I to Oxford, the headquarters of the Royalists. It is recorded that Sir Frederick behaved gallantly in many of the actions of the Civil War, and his tireless good-humour was of great encouragement to the King. Unhappily, his wife, the Lady Elizabeth, died whilst they were at Oxford, in 1643, and was buried there in Christ Church Cathedral. So the children at Culford became motherless, and the infrequent, but always longed-for visits of their charming mother were no more.

Life went on very much the same at Culford. Anne, Lady Jane's eldest daughter, had married Sir Thomas Meautys, her mother's cousin. He must have been much older than his bride, who was twenty-five when she married him. It is possible that she met very few eligible young men in the quiet of the country, and Cousin Meautys had a wonderful home and was comfortably off. He had been the confidential friend and secretary to the great Lord Chancellor, Sir Francis Bacon who had given to Sir Thomas his mansion of Gorhambury which had been built by Sir Francis's father, Sir Nicholas Bacon, before he became Lord Keeper. Whether this was a marriage of convenience or whether Anne had grown fond of her mother's cousin, we do not know, but she bore him one daughter, Jane, who was baptised at Culford on the 13th of October, 1641. About this time Lady Jane received a letter from her sister-in-law, Anne, Lady Meautys, the mother of Hercules Meautys.

19 Maye, 1641.

. . . . I understand by Mr Meautys's ancient my niece is married, I pray God make her happie, and I doe sincerely wish that all things may fall out to your contentment. . . .

and also,

Deare Sister,

In my other letters I did desire yo to send us over ye monie, wch, if y^o please, should bee very wellcome unto us. Thus, wishing much happiness vnto y^o and yours,

I remaine redy to doe y^o servise in all true affection to my end,

Anne Meautys.

ye 9th of June 1636.

Deare Sister, if y° please, send mee word how my Hercules doth, to whome I send my blessing.

To the Lady Bacon, at Culford.

We are not told if "tyme" had altered the "wildness" in Hercules, nor do we know what became of him.

Lady Jane's charges were all growing up, when, on the 7th of October, 1647, another baby was baptised at Culford. She was Jane, "ye daughter of Sir Fredericke Cornwallis", who had lately married, as his second wife, Elizabeth, the daughter of Sir Henry Croftes of Little Saxham, Suffolk, and grand-daughter of Sir John Croftes of West Stow Hall.

Two years later, in October 1649, Sir Thomas Meautys, Lady Jane's cousin and son-in-law died, and shortly afterwards his widow the Lady Anne married Sir Harbottle Grimston, Baronet; he was forty-seven and she thirty-three. Sir Harbottle, whose first wife was Mary, the daughter of Sir George Croke, had been M.P. for Colchester from 1640-8, and before Sir Thomas Meautys died had purchased Gorhambury from him for £10,000. It would seem to have been convenient for both parties to marry since Gorhambury had been the home of the Lady Anne and her first husband. Lady Anne bore Sir Harbottle an only daughter, Anna, who was baptised "ye 12 day of October, 1652", but on the "7 day of Aprill" of the same year, her little Jane, the child of her first husband, died, aged ten years. Anna, the second child, only lived to be four, dying on the 21st May, 1657. This poor little girl was buried near the altar in Culford Church and there is an inscription on her tombstone: "Anne Grimstone, ye daughter of Sir Harbottle Grimstone Baronett and Dame Anne his wife, departed this life the 21 day of May, Anno Domi 1657, being of ye age of 4 yeares, seven months, 2 weekes and three days. She was a child of lovely hope, ye joy of her parents, and wanted nothing but Heaven to make her happy, where she is now, cloathed with immortality and crowned with eternity."

Meanwhile, Charles Cornwallis, Sir Frederick's son and heir, whom Lady Bacon had looked after since childhood, had married Margaret Playsted, of Arlington, and his first child, Frederick, was baptised on the 13th of July 1652, when Charles was aged twenty. Subsequently, Charles and his wife produced eleven children, but five of them died very young; Frederick died on July 17th, 1655, and a girl, Anne, was buried ten days earlier. These two are buried in the nave of Culford Church, next to each other. Then there was Nathaniel, who was buried in 1656, aged three years, and Elizabeth, buried in 1664, and James, baptised in November, and buried in December of the same year 1664. The other six of Charles Cornwallis's children, including Charles the third child, who became the third Lord, were all baptised at Culford, and presumably born in the Hall, though Brome Hall was still used by Lady Jane's family, and it is possible that Sir Frederick used it as a home for his new wife.

If this was so, Sir Frederick did not enjoy the beauty of Brome for long. He had always been a staunch Royalist, and when Charles II fled from Cromwell's men to the Continent, Sir Frederick followed him, and in company with a small group of other noble lords he shared the King's poverty and exile for eight long years.

His mother was growing old. She had lived a full life, if not an exciting one. She had had friends at Court, had been a personal friend of Charles I's sister, and had walked herself in the King's coronation procession. She had lived through the years of the Civil War, with her son often in danger following the Royalist cause, she had brought up so many children, had been present at the baptisms of many grand-children, and great-grand-children, and alas, at their funerals as well. In 1653, Mr John Fenne, an old retainer and friend of the family, who had been well-liked by Sir Nathaniel, had died, and so another link with her youth was broken. She had been a careful manager of her estates and lands, and was most anxious, as may be seen in her Will, that the farms should be well-tended and maintained, and that her houses should not be allowed to fall into ruin. She had lived to know of the execution of a King, the King who had befriended her son, and whose consort had bequeathed lands to herself, and now, that King's son was King, but in exile, and her son was absent with him.

Looking back over the years it must have seemed a long time since she came as a bride to Culford, and as was the custom in those days, she ordered her tomb. It was to be made in Culford Church by Thomas Stanton of Holborn, the stonemason who had executed the bust of Sir Nathaniel Bacon in the west porch of the Church. The agreement reads:

. . . . before the 1st of August, 1658, to well and artificially make, cut out and carve, according to the best skill of a stonecutter, alle in whit and blacke marble, and toucht fine polichte, to be of the height of tenn foote fromme toppe to bottom and in breadth seaven foote. . . .

The charge for the making of this tomb was to be £300, which would be a great sum in those days, and Lady Jane gave the order in August 1657. The following spring she sent for her lawyer and while the log fire smouldered in the hearth of the Hall, and the chill east wind whistled down the chimney, she made her will.

I Dame Jane Bacon of Culford in the County of Suffolk late wife of Sir Nathaniel Bacon late of Culford aforesayd Knight of the Bath deceased and before the wife of Sir William Cornwallis late of Brome in the sayd County deceased, Doe ordeine and make this my last will and testament in manner following. First I will my body shalbe buried in Christian buriall in the Chancell of the parish Church of Culford afore sayd soe neere my sayd late husband Sir Nathaniel Bacon as may conveniently be, Without any pomp or solemne funerall early in the morning and not in the Night att which I desyre that a sermon maybe, And many of my children and grand children be present as conveniently may, and I will that a devout monument or Tombe if not made in my life be made for me in such manner as I have given Directions to my Executors, I alsoe will that a devout monument or Tombe shall be made in the Chancell of the parish Church of Ockley in the sayd County for the sayd Sir William Cornewallis and both his wives, viz, His first wife the Lady Lucy one of the daughters and coheyres of Sir John Nevill Knight Lord Latymer and myselfe and all the children of the sayd Sir William and alsoe one other monument or Tombe of playne stone for William Cornewallis Esquire, Great-Grandfather of the sayd Sir William which I will shall not exceed together the charge of one hundred pounds, Then I will that all my children grandchildren Executors Doctor Buckenham my Phisitian and my servants shall have blackes for mourninges according to their severall degrees att the discresion of my Executors, Then I doe give and bequeath to the poor people of Brome aforesayd Fourteen pounds, To the poor of Ockley aforesayd fourteen pounds, to the poor of Stuston twelve pounds, to the poore of Thrandiston twelve pounds, To the poore of Palgrave fourteen pounds, To the poore of Thorpe Cornwallis alias Thorpe Abbot Four pounds, To the poore of Osmondiston alias Scole in Norfolk four poundes, To the poore of Wilton in Cleaveland in the County of Yorke five pounds, To the poore of Culford aforesayd Teen pounds, To the poore of Ingham Teen pounds, To the poore of Tymworth Teen pounds, All which sumes of money I will shall be payd into the hands of the Churchwardens and overseers of the poore for the tyme beinge of the same severall parishes respectively to be by them distributed by the advice of the minister and chief inhabitants of the same parishes respectively, Soe that it may be noe hinderance to their weekly or monthly collection to be made accordinge to the statute, For I intend to relieve the poore and not to spare the purses of the rich.

Culford Hall was to be held in trust for Nicholas Bacon, her son, now married, for his use for life, "and all my pictures which were the late Sir Nathaniel Bacon and all my other pictures at Culford, and all my stules and chayres which were Sir Nicholas Bacon and my hangings, householdestuffe and implements of household and lynnon in or about my house in Culford". . . .
"And I will that an inventory of the sayd Pictures hangings and premises shall be taken within twoe monthes after my decease one part thereof to remayne with my Executors and the other parte with the sayd Nicholas Bacon and that once every yeare a viewe be taken of them and the inventories examined and made right and let my Executors and the survivour of them by the same inventory after the death of the sayd Nicholas Bacon shall deliver over the sayd pictures hangings and premises to such person and persons to whom my sayd house by me is limited and appointed there to remayne to the uses aforesayd and to be as heyreloomes to my sayd house." Nicholas was also to have "my coach and coachhorses with their furniture my silver basin and the sealls att armes which were his father's and my little round leather boxe with three and thirty pistols of gold and my little silver boxe with little amber bottles which he gave me", and to "Elizabeth Bacon my daughter-in-law the summe of one hundred pounds". Nicholas Bacon also received the "proffits and benefitts" arising from the upkeep of the farms and estates of Culford, Ingham and Tymworth.

Sir Frederick, for whom his mother had already paid £13,000 in settlement of his debts, was to receive a considerable annuity from the Culford Estate and a yearly sum of £500 from her other manors, and after provision had been made for her grandchildren and great-grandchildren's "educacion" the greater part of the rest of Lady Jane's manors, halls and lands, including the Cornwallis ancestral home of Brome Hall, were left in trust for Sir Frederick for his life, and to the Cornwallis line after him.

Lady Jane bequeathed many personal items to various relatives and friends; to her daughter, Dame Anne Grimston, she left £1,000 and also "my childbed lynnon, my furres, my watch, my alarum, my bloodstone, my Egge of the Lady Kent's powder (Pomander?), my white and black callicoe curtains vallance and counterpoint, to the same belonginge and bedstead and stules and my chayres and other things of the same suite". All Lady Jane's "papers and writing's" concerning Culford Hall were also to be left in the care of Dame Anne Grimston.

The "divers manors Granges lands and tenements" bequeathed to Dame Jane by "The excellent Princess Heneretta Maria late Queene of England" were left in trust for her grandchild Frederick Cornwallis and his heirs after him.

Miss Dorothy Randolph, Lady Jane's "cosin" who had tried to help her find the right kind of wife for Sir Frederick so many years ago, received "my aggitt ringe", there was an annuity of five pounds for Mrs Parr, the widow of the Rev. Elnathan Parr of Palgrave, who had acted as go-between for Nathaniel and Jane before they became engaged. There were legacies for all the personal servants at Culford, and one half year's wages to all other servants at the Hall, and instructions that they should be entertained freely at Culford for two months after Lady Jane's decease, "with such provision for housekeeping as I shall leave in my house att Culford".

> Item, I give and bequeath unto Mr Jeames Warwell and his wife five poundes to buy a piece of plate in remembrance of me and to Mr Martyne Norrige of Culford Clerke (Whom I desyre should preach att my funerall) Twenty pounds and a mourneing gowen and to his wife five poundes to buy a piece of plate, Item I give and bequeath to my servants hereafter named these legacies followinge. That is to say, To Edward Voyce my Chaplein twenty pounds, And my will is and I doe earnestly desyre, That he may be presented to the next living shall be voyd and in the gift of eyther of my sonnes or of my

Executors, to John Goldsmyth twenty poundes, To Thomas Nelson twenty poundes, To Jasper Spaldinge ten poundes To John Warren teen poundes, To Willm Girlinge to Tabitha Brewster twenty poundes, to Mary Jackson three poundes and to every other of my servants that shall be dwellinge with me at my death (except William Randolph whom I have lately retayned) one halfe yeares wages respectively over and above such wages as shall be due to them. And my will and meaninge is, That all my servants in household shall have entertaynement according to there severall degrees att Culford aforesayd by the space of twoe monthes after my decease with such provision for housekeeping as I shall leave in my house att Culford aforesayd and the rest of the charge to be borne by my Executors out of my personal estate.

The Executors appointed were Charles Cornwallis "my Grand-child", Sir Harbottle Grimston "my sonne in law", Charles Cornwallis "my kinsman", and Edmond Hervey, Esquire. The first three of these each received two hundred pounds, and Edmond Hervey two hundred and fifty pounds.

In May of the following year, 1659, Lady Bacon died. She was seventy-nine years old, and was buried in the chancel of Culford Church as she desired in front of the "devout monument" which she had had made; it is considered to be amongst Thomas Stanton's finest work, showing her seated in a chair holding her daughter's child, Anna Grimston, on her knee, her own little daughter Jane, who had died aged three, and her daughter's other child, Jane Meautys, who had died aged ten, both standing at her right hand; and at her left, Anne, Frederick, and Nathaniel Cornwallis, three of her great-grandchildren, who died in infancy. If any satisfaction is to be had from seeing one's own monument in the Church where one expects to be buried, then Lady Jane had that satisfaction, but the joy of seeing her son home again from exile was never hers, for she died before he returned. Presumably her other son, Sir Nicholas Bacon, and her daughter Lady Anne Grimston came to Culford for their mother's funeral on this sad May morning and even though she had desired no pomp or solemnity, there would still be a large gathering, with grand-children and the great-grandchildren, all the Culford men-servants in their "blackes for mourneing", and many a friend of the family and many a humble villager waiting to pay his last respects to one who had lived amongst them for almost a lifetime.

After it was all over and Mr Martin Norridge had preached the sermon which Lady Jane had desired, he made this simple entry in the Parish Register:

The Lady Jane Bacon was buryed the 24th of May, 1659

How strange Culford must have seemed without her.

In the following January, Nicholas Bacon, who never seemed to enjoy much prosperity, and had at one time been imprisoned for a debt of £600, died at the early age of forty-three. There is no record of Lady Jane paying his debt for him, whereas she paid thousands of pounds for Sir Frederick. It does seem that Frederick was the favourite son. Nicholas was described as "a man of great modesty", he became M.P. for Ipswich, and was knighted in 1627. When he died without issue in 1660, his effigy was added to his mother's monument. He is shown lying full length at her feet with his head resting on his right hand and holding a book in his left.

In the year 1660, also, Charles II returned from exile, and Sir Frederick Cornwallis came back with him. On the 20th April, he was with much pomp and ceremony created Baron Cornwallis of Eye and Treasurer of His Majesty's Household. He was, by this time, a florid, amiable-looking man, as a portrait hanging in Audley End, Essex, shows. Returning to Brome and Culford from the scene of his triumph in London, he found not only his mother dead, but his stepbrother also. Of the four children born to his first wife Elizabeth, only Charles remained, the other three, Frederick (whose daughter Jane by his wife Anne Barber married in Paris on 14th May 1682 Anthony Dunscombe, the Governor of Scarborough Castle), George, and Henrietta Maria, named after Charles I's Queen, were all dead. It must have been a great comfort to him to be reunited to his second wife Elizabeth, and their young daughter Jane, now fourteen years old. The quiet house, at Brome, where his step-father had once planted white roses, was his by right, and because Nicholas, Sir Nathaniel's son, had left no heir, Culford, serenely peaceful with its Hall, and farms, and the Church where his mother and so many of the family lay at rest, became his too. Alas, it was not for long; he died of apoplexy in January 1662 and was buried at Brome, but his children and his children's children and their children after them continued to live at Culford for nearly two hundred years.

6   A New Chapter

CHARLES, second Lord Cornwallis, was one of the four children of Sir Frederick Cornwallis and his first wife Elizabeth Ashburnham, who had been brought up at Culford by their grandmother, whilst their father and mother were living at the court of Charles I. He was born at Culford and baptised there on 19th April 1632. His grandmother's home-loving influence must have been great, since the boy scarcely saw his father, and his mother died when he was twelve. He appears to have grown into a most reliable man; his grandmother nominated him one of her executors and referred to him several times in her will as though he were the person in whom she could trust most of all. Sir Henry Croftes, son of Sir John Croftes of West Stow Hall, also appointed him an executor of his will, referring to Lord Cornwallis as "my very worthy friend". Sir Henry Croftes' daughter Elizabeth was the second wife of Sir Frederick Cornwallis, Lord Charles' father, so there was a close connection between the two families.

Lord Charles married Margaret, the daughter of Thomas Playsted of Arlington. He must have been about nineteen years old at the time since he was only twenty when their first child, a boy named Frederick, was born in July 1652. The following year Nathaniel was born, and then Anne. These three children all died within two years and are the three depicted on the left of their great-grandmother, Lady Jane Bacon, in the monument set up in the Chancel of Culford Church. Charles and his wife produced eleven children before she died in 1668, only six surviving. Charles, the third Lord, was born on 28th December, 1655, Henrietta Maria in October 1657; she lived until October 1707 and was buried at Fornham All Saints; her great-grandmother, Lady Jane Bacon left her "the summe of six hundred pounds." A second Frederick was born in November 1658, William in March 1661, Thomas baptised at Culford in April 1663, and George, baptised in November 1666. Two years later, Margaret, Lady Cornwallis, died and was buried in Culford Church, where there is a memorial placed on the south wall of the porch to her memory. Lord Charles lived only five years after his wife died. In the year following her death 1669, we find his name mentioned in connection with the trial in Bury St Edmunds of the "Lowestoft Witches", two poor women named Amy Derry and Rose Cullender. . . . "Several gentlemen were dissatisfied with the evidence, upon which an experiment to see whether the afflicted children recognised blindfold Amy Derry's touch, having failed, Lord Cornwallis, Sir Edmund Bacon, a great-nephew of Sir Nicholas who built Culford Hall, Sgt. Keeling and others openly declared that they did believe the whole transaction of this business was a mere imposture. But Mr Pacy's (a dissenting minister) arguments and those of the learned Dr Brown prevailed. Judge Hall summed up and the prisoners were condemmed to be hanged". His Lordship's protests could not save the poor wretches.

Perhaps he brought his kinsman Sir Edmund Bacon home to Culford that day, where they discussed the trial over a meal before Sir Edmund rode back to Redgrave, still the home of the Bacons.

Lord Cornwallis must have been a quiet, retiring man. He was made a Knight of the Bath in 1661, at the Restoration of Charles II and before he died he was made a Privy Counsellor, but not a great deal is known about him.

At his death he was buried by his wife's side in Culford Church beneath the memorial which he had placed there. The memorial takes the form of a long double tablet, the right side recording the death of the Lady Margaret, with the names of the six children who survived her, and those of the five she had lost. It was evidently intended that the left-hand panel should record the death of her husband, but when he died in April, 1673 at the early age of forty-one, his sons and daughters raised no memorial to his name.

A young man of eighteen next became Lord of the Manor of Culford.

Charles, third son of Lord Charles, baptised in December 1655, was evidently a Christmas baby, born whilst the keen wind blew across the frozen lake and there was noise and laughter in the kitchens as the maids and men were preparing to keep Christmas. The old grandmother, Lady Jane who was still alive and very much the mistress of Culford, saw to it that all was done for the comfort of Lady Margaret, and that Doctor Buckenham, "my Phisitian" was brought in to the great log fire in the hall and treated handsomely when he informed his Lordship that another son was born.

But when this baby grew up, he was not at all the steady, respected man that his father had been. He fell in love with Elizabeth the daughter of Sir Stephen Fox, a very rich and very shrewd man who subsequently became Paymaster-General and had much to do with the building of the Royal Hospital, Chelsea. After the death of his father the second Lord Cornwallis, in April, Charles, now the third Baron Cornwallis of Eye, married Mistress Elizabeth on 27th December of the same year, 1673. They were both eighteen, and the wedding took place in Westminster Abbey, an important social event, since Sir Stephen Fox was Treasurer of the Household to Charles II whom he had always served faithfully, and the Cornwallis family had enjoyed Royal favour for years.

Lady Elizabeth became the mother of four sons, Charles, William, James and John. Charles, who eventually inherited the Cornwallis title and estates from his father, was born in 1675, presumably at Brome, as there is no record of his birth in the Culford register.

For some time after his marriage to Elizabeth Fox, Culford saw little of its new Lord. He was a spendthrift, a gambler, and a great lover of life at Court; country life seemed to have had little appeal for him. In fact he did, for a time, lend Culford Hall to the Duke of York, later to become James II. In a Subsidy List for Suffolk for 1674, namely the hated "Hearth Tax", the Hall is described as having twenty-nine chimneys, classed as "Empty", and listed under the name "The Duke of Yorke". The only record of the Duke's sojourn at Culford which it has been possible to trace is contained in a letter dated 21st March, 1675, from Sir Robert Carr, saying "The Duke has gone to Culford, I have sent his letter after him".

It may have been convenient for the Royal Duke to borrow Culford Hall in order to be near his brother the King when he stayed at Euston Hall after racing at Newmarket, or to use as his head-quarters when hunting in Thetford Chase, but he seems not to have made great use of the place. On one occasion, however, when Charles II was visiting his friend and equerry Edward Proger of West Stow Hall, Culford was the scene of a Royal scandal. The story is told that the King and his party rode over from West Stow to see Lord Charles Cornwallis, and presumably the Duke of York. There was a great deal of drinking and merrymaking, and as the day was a Sunday, one of the party preached a mock sermon to amuse the King. At this, the Rector, the Reverend Martin Norridge, who had been Rector in Dame Bacon's time, was brought in and requested to fetch his daughter Elizabeth, a girl of twenty-one, to meet His Majesty. This the Rector did, but if the story is true he must have bitterly regretted that day's work. We are not told what happened when the King and the girl were alone, but afterwards she was so panic-stricken that she took her own life by "jumping from a height", probably from a window of the Hall. It is certainly true that Elizabeth was "buryed May 23, 1674". Maybe it was for this reason that Culford Hall stood empty for a time, there being too much gossip and ill-will for it to be a healthy place for the King's relations and friends.

Whilst the "Duke of Yorke" was the occupier of Culford Hall, the notorious Charles, whose wife was having her family at Brome, was living an almost dissipated life in London; so much so that in 1678 after a drunken brawl he was charged with the murder of a boy-soldier named Robert Clarke. Lord Cornwallis and a friend of his named Gerrard became involved in an argument with some young soldiers in Whitehall and were so infuriated that Gerrard threw the boy Clarke to the ground, killing him instantly. Both men were accused of murder, but His Lordship was tried by his Peers in the Court of the Lord High Steward and found not guilty; the other man, at his trial pleaded the King's Pardon and was released.

In 1679 Charles and Elizabeth's second son, William, died, and the year after that the young Lady Elizabeth herself died at the age of twenty-five. She was buried at the little Church near Brome Hall, their country home, where her wealthy father, Sir Stephen Fox built a row of alms houses, which are still standing. About this time, Sir Stephen also rebuilt Culford Church, of which more will be said later.

Probably his young wife's death subdued Lord Charles, for no more is heard of him until 1688 when he married again, this time the Lady Anne Scott, Duchess of Monmouth and Buccleuch, who was the widow of James, Duke of Monmouth. By her he had three more children, Lord George Scott, Lady Anne, and Lady Isabella.

When Lady Anne became Lady of the Manor of Culford, she seems to have set about putting the place in order after its period of emptiness. For in a "Book of Accts: 1689-1692" may be found these items:

		£	s	d
	Paid for repairs at Culford Hall 1689-1691-1692	781	13	8
	Charges about Brome Hall and Culford Gardens in 1689	485	19	1½
	Paid charges of Brickmaking	191	16	0
	Paid Madam Henrietta Cornwallis Annuity	320	19	11
1689 Jan. 9	To Mr Ross, 1 yr's salary for the molecatcher and sexton at Culford due Michelmas last	1	10	0
1689	To Jim Rust for charcoal	19	10	0
1692	Spent on meat at Brome and Culford	152	0	0

These items are most interesting, and if one looks at the yearly salary paid to Mr Ross perhaps equation with today's values becomes more apparent. Evidently the repairs to Culford Hall were considerable, involving quite an amount of new bricks, and it is extremely interesting to see what an amount of money was spent on the gardens, once the delight of the Bacons and now laid out anew in splendour. Moles were as much trouble to the gardeners of Culford in those days as they are today, but there is no longer a Jim Rust who supplies charcoal. "Madam Henrietta Cornwallis" who received the annuity was Lord Cornwallis's younger sister. She was two years his junior, never married, and was buried at Fornham All Saints, Suffolk, in 1707. Her tomb stands outside the East Window and can be seen, but is in a decayed state.

This lady not only pulled Culford together, she seems to have also pulled together her husband, for he started to take an active part in public life, and in the year 1689 he was made Lord Lieutenant of Suffolk. In 1691 he was called to the Privy Council and became First Lord of the Admiralty from 1692-1693.

No doubt the fact of his becoming First Lord accounts for the large meat bills at Brome Hall and Culford in 1692, since more entertaining was being undertaken. Quite likely the scene at Culford was more splendid now that it had been since the Elizabethan days of Sir Nicholas Bacon.

His life was short, as his father's and grandfather's before him; he died when he was forty-three, on the 29th April, 1698, and was laid to rest near his first wife in the quiet Church at Brome on the 6th May. A peaceful haven for one who, but for the accident of birth, might have hanged for murder at Tyburn.

Quiet Interlude

THE pattern of life at Culford in the early eighteenth century was very quiet and domesticated, compared with the eventful lives of the Cornwallises of the seventeenth century.

Mr Martin Norridge, who had been Rector for close on thirty-eight years, died in 1684 and was buried in Culford Church, where there is a slate slab on the chancel steps above his resting place. The Rev. James Davies was Rector when the fourth Lord inherited Culford. He was Charles, the eldest of the four sons of Elizabeth Fox, the first wife of the notorious third Lord Cornwallis. He was born in 1675 and became a soldier as his ancestors had been. On the 6th of June, 1699, at St Martin-in-the-Fields, he married Lady Charlotte Butler, the daughter and heir of the Earl of Arran. As with all the eldest sons of the Cornwallis family, he was able to secure a seat in Parliament as Member for Eye, Suffolk from 1695-1698.

He and his lady produced twelve children, nine sons and three daughters, only two of whom were baptised at Culford, the Honble. Stephen, baptised "ye first day of January One Thousand seven hundred and Three"; and the Honble. Charlot, who was baptised on the eleventh of November, 1704, and buried on the 22nd of April, 1705.

This Lord served his country and county faithfully and well, he was Lord Lieutenant of Suffolk from 1698-1703, and became LL.D. of Cambridge University in October 1717.

His seventh son, Frederick, became Archbishop of Canterbury, and was a greatly loved and revered prelate; he evidently resembled his father, of whom it was said that "he was a gentleman of sweet disposition, well esteemed in his native county of Suffolk. He was of fair complexion, inclining to fat." This fair complexion and tendency to fatness was a characteristic of the Cornwallises, and it is noticeable that the fourth Lord, as so many of his predecessors, died very young, being in his forty-seventh year; the entry in the Register reads:

1721

Buried ye Right Honble. Charles Lord Cornwallis jan. 27th. 1720/1/2, his coffin stands upon his Grandfather's wch is just 7 foot into ground.

His wife died five years later on 19th August, 1725, and was buried near her husband. There are slabs in the Baptistry of Culford Church recording their burials.

There is also the entry of the burial of Captain James Cornwallis, the second son of the fourth Lord; we are told that:

. . . .he died May ye 27, 1727 in Copenhagen Road in ye 26t year of his age beloved by all who had ye Honr to know him.

The twin brother of the Hon. Frederick Cornwallis, Archbishop of Canterbury, was the Hon. Edward, who founded the town of Halifax in Nova Scotia in 1748, and eventually became Governor of Gibraltar, where he died. He was brought to Culford for burial, and the entry in the Register reads:

The Honorable Edward Cornwallis Lieutenant General and Governor of Gibraltar aged 62, born March 5th 1713, died Jan. 14 1776.

As boys, the twins, Frederick and Edward, were reputed to be so alike that it was difficult to tell them apart. They were made royal pages at the tender age of twelve years, but at eighteen Edward entered the army, and thereafter their lives followed very different paths; but there seemed to be an affinity between them to the end.

The eldest son, Charles, born on 29th March, 1701, succeeded his father as Lord of the Manor. He seems to have taken an active part in the affairs of his day, but appears not to have represented Eye in the House of Commons as the Cornwallis heirs before him had done, possibly because he was twenty-one when his father died and he would go straight to the House of Lords as Baron Cornwallis of Eye. He was made Groom of the Bedchamber to George I on 19th August, 1721, and on the 28th November, 1722, at St James, Westminster, he married Elizabeth, the eldest daughter of Viscount Townshend. Their first child was a girl, Elizabeth, born on 1st September, 1723, possibly in London, but brought to Culford to be baptised on 1st October. On 4th January, 1725, the

Honble. Louisa, their second daughter was buried. Two years later another daughter was born on 13th October, 1727, named Lucy, but she died four days later and was buried in the Church at Culford; there is a slab in the West Porch bearing her name. Not all the wealth and comfort of the nobility could save so many of their children, but Mary, the fourth girl, was baptised at Culford on the 6th June, 1736, and survived until she lost her own life in childbirth thirty-four years later. She married Samuel Whitbread the brewer in 1769 and died the year following. On 31st December, 1738, was born "at his Lordships House in Grosvenor Square, London", Charles, the eldest son. Two years later Henry was born; James was born at "his Ld.Shps House in Dover Street, Lond, Feb 25t, 1743," and in February, 1744 William was born. Charles, James and William all became men of importance; Henry died when twenty-one.

The family lived a great deal of their time in London now, and Culford Hall became their country house. In 1740 Lord Charles was made Constable of the Tower of London, and in 1753 he was created an Earl by the title of Viscount Brome in the County of Suffolk and Earl Cornwallis thus bringing great honour to his family. Nevertheless, his Lordship was not disinterested in his country home. In the year 1742 he had the park surveyed and planned by the landscape gardener Thomas Wright, whose plan is in the Record Office at Bury St Edmunds. It may have been Thomas Wright who planted the lime trees at Culford —he was noted for his love of limes and planted many in different towns— and it is most likely that to him we owe the lovely limes on the South Front, which exude such an intoxicating fragrance in the evenings of early summer.

In that age of elegant manners and picturesque costume, the age of George II, when it was fashionable to cultivate "pastoral" pursuits, the lords and ladies of Culford and their friends, the ladies dressed like Dresden shepherdesses in delicate silks and satins, the men in flowered waistcoats and richly embroidered coats, spent many a drowsy summer afternoon idly chatting and gossiping beneath the trees on the lawn to the south of the Hall. For here was the perfect setting for this pastoral life, with pleasant neighbours at all the great houses and halls around, so that the days could be passed in gathering wild flowers, or in "strawberry gatherings", whilst the evenings were given to cards and music, or to dancing in the softly flattering light of candles.

Amongst these visitors to Culford were Spencer Cowper, the Dean of Durham from 1746-1774, and his wife; he was the cousin of William Cowper the poet, and a relative by marriage of Lord Cornwallis. The late Professor Edward Hughes of the University of Durham kindly supplied a letter of the Dean's, dated 15th August, 1752, written from Brome; it is interesting to see that whilst Brome Hall was still owned by Lord Cornwallis, Culford was used almost exclusively by the family as a country house:—

Broome, Aug. 15th, 1752.

. . . .Monday evening we reached Cambridge, and next day St Edmundsbury, one of the prettiest, and the very cleanest Town I ever saw. In our way to it we saw Culford Hall, Lord Cornwallis's other seat, a sweet place, its scituation clean and dry like Colegreen, and its park not unlike, but with the advantage of a fine piece of water in the front of the House, wch extends in curve for half a mile, but is not seen in front above one third of it; the rest lost amongst the Trees. The House is somewhat like Ld. King's at Ockham, and stands in the Park witht. any garden round it. As Culford is the Favourite nothing is done here, but just preserving the house from wind and weather. . . .

After he became Earl Cornwallis his Lordship continued to make improvements at Culford, building a laundry and wash-house, a dairy, and a stable and coach house. Below is printed a copy of the old Insurance Policy for these buildings, all insured for only £1,000 —

POLICY NO. 178559.   DATED — 21st Octor. 1760.
PREMIUM — £1. 4. —.   RENEWAL DATE — MICHS. 1761.

A G E N T
Johnson.

The Right Honble. Charles Earl Cornwallis of
Culford in the County of Suffolk On his Laundry
& Washouse only adjoining each other & two
rooms over the Laundry Situated in Culford
aforesaid Plaister & Tiled not Exceeding Two
Hundred Pounds   200

Dairy & Backhouse adjoining each other & Rooms
over the same with a Brewhouse & Chamber
adjoining thereto distant from the Laundry Clay
& Tiled not Exceeding Two Hundred Pounds   200

& on a large Stable & Coach house adjoining each
other with Granaries & Rooms over the same Brick
& Tiled not Exceeding Six Hundred Pounds   600
                                                    ————
                                                    £1,000
                                                    ————

The laundry referred to has disappeared but the large stable
and coach house were the buildings now used as a garage and an
art room, the doors of the loft and the granary can be seen on the
upper storey, and the building is marked on a map of the period.
Culford in the eighteenth century was beginning to assume the
shape that we know to-day.

Meanwhile the Earl's sons were becoming men and taking up
their careers. The eldest, Charles, was a soldier, the youngest,
William, joined the Navy, and James, the third son, who was a
scholar, entered the Church.

The Earl wrote to his son, the Hon. William, from Culford in
June, 1761, ". . . .I am very sensible it must be more expensive
to you now you are a Lieutenant. I am very willing to allow what
is necessary to you, and would by no means have you live worse
than your brother officers. I suppose you will not be able to do
with less than a hundred a year. . . ."

A "hundred a year" went a great deal further then than it
does to-day. About the same time Lady Cornwallis's housekeeper
entered in her Book of Accounts . . . . "Paid a helpe in ye laundry
. . . .8d." She did not state whether the payment was for a week
or a day!

This Lord of the Manor of Culford lived longer than his forbears, departing this life on 23rd June, 1762, in his sixty-third
year at Bristol. He was brought to Culford for burial in the
family vault on 2nd July. His widow, Elizabeth Countess
Cornwallis survived him twenty-three years, until she was eighty-
five, when she too was buried in Culford Church. The Dowager
Countess was a regular correspondent of her son William, and
numerous letters of hers have been preserved, many of them of a

political flavour; she seems to have left no stone unturned in order to further her son's advantage, as, for instance, a letter to the Hon. William in August 1763 ". . . .Lord Halifax. . . .gave me an absolute promise he will make you a Post Captain. . . there are none of my friends in town, so I can get no secret intelligence how things go on, but this is certain, that Mr Pitt was alone with the King from 12 to 3 at yest. noon Buckingham House". The Hon. William eventually became Admiral Cornwallis, but his mother did not live to see that day. In September of the same year she again wrote to William that ". . . .your Brother (the new Lord) is at last got to Culford, and James, Fellow of Merton, by this time with him." (James was very pleased at having been made a Fellow of his College at Oxford.)

In the year 1764, the Hon. William's ship was badly damaged, and the family feared for his life; his mother wrote:—

Oct. 19th. . . . "I was so fortunate not to hear of the accident that befell you till I had it from your brother, who had a great deal of company at Culford and was informed by Admiral Keppel. . . .Molly* wrote from Culford to me."

The Right Honourable Charles, second Earl Cornwallis, keeping "a great deal of company at Culford", was at this time nearly twenty-six years old. He had been born in London on the last day of 1738, and was educated at Eton College. He was hit in the eye during a hockey match there, and as a result his sight was permanently affected. He was later sent to the Military Academy of Turin, and passed out as a professional soldier when he was eighteen years old. Now his father was dead and he was Earl Cornwallis, and destined to be the most noteworthy of them all. Later in life he was to long only for the peace which Culford could afford, and to resent unnecessary visitors, but now, in his youth, he was enjoying entertaining his friends in his own home, discussing with them the political affairs of the day, and showing off the park in its autumn glory.

*Lady Mary Cornwallis, sister to Charles, William and James.

(i) The first Culford Hall built for Sir Nicholas Bacon in red brick in 1591.

(ii) Considerable alterations were made to the Hall in 1790/93 for the first Marquis Cornwallis, and in 1806 a portico was added for the second Marquis Cornwallis.

(iii)   Aerial view of the north face of Culford Hall as it is to-day.

(iv)   The south face of the Hall to-day with the original block on the left and to which the steps lead.

(v) The main staircase in the Georgian part of Culford Hall with portrait of the first Earl Cadogan on the right.

The Times of London

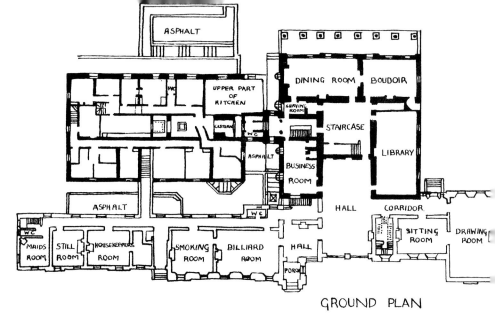

GROUND PLAN

5 0 10 20 30 40 50 60 70 FEET

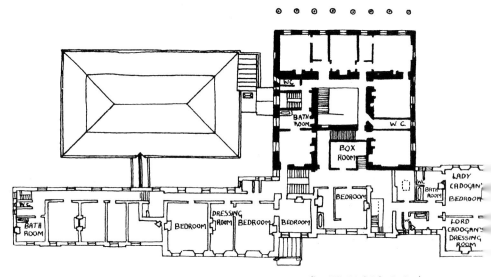

FIRST FLOOR PLAN

(vi)   Plan of alterations to Culford Hall copied by Philip Wyndham from the drawing by William Young, the architect.

(vii) The lake at Culford Hall.

Nigel Salmon

(viii) The stone bridge built for the fifth Earl Cadogan on the iron base originally supporting the bridge made for the first Marquis Cornwallis. This used to be the main approach to the Hall over the heath from the Newmarket Lodge.

(x)   First Marquis Cornwallis.

(ix)   Self-portrait of Sir Nathaniel Bacon.

(xi) Lieutenant General Cadogan, later first Earl Cadogan, and the Duke of Marlborough at Malplaquet.

by kind permission of Lord Cadogan

(xii) Tomb of Jane, Lady Bacon, and at her feet her son, Sir Nicholas.

(xiii) The Boleyn Gate.

(xiv) Church of St Mary, Culford.

8   The Marquisate 1762-1823

WHEN Charles, the second Earl Cornwallis came to possess Culford, a little over a hundred years after the death of his capable ancestress Lady Jane Bacon, the house and the grounds were much the same as she had left them; the park had been re-planned, as has been stated, the Church had been re-built, but the village still clustered round the Church, the lake was the same size as when Sir Nicholas Bacon first dug "the greate pond" in 1624, and apart from the new stables and the laundry built by the first Earl there was little difference to be seen. To this country home Lord Cornwallis brought his bride in January 1768. She was the daughter of Colonel James Jones, and they were married at St George's, Hanover Square, on the 14th of July; no doubt a fashionable wedding of the day, for Lord Cornwallis was by this time Aide-de-Camp to George III and a Groom of the Bedchamber to His Majesty. His Lordship was thirty years old when he married Mistress Jemima, who was twenty-one; she was a sad-looking though beautiful young woman, happy at Culford when her husband was with her, but grieving sorrowfully when his duties as a soldier took him away from home. Their first child was a little girl, Mary, and the heir, Charles, Viscount Brome, was baptised at Culford on 24th October, 1774.

Before this little boy was two years old, war broke out with America, and Cornwallis was given the Command of a Division of the British Army. His wife was so upset at his going, that she prevailed upon his Uncle Frederick, the Archbishop of Canterbury, to persuade the King to allow Lord Cornwallis to return home and relinquish his command. Although His Grace secured this permission, Cornwallis refused to comply with his wife's wishes. He was a man of strong principles, a soldier from his youth, and it was anathema to him to even think of giving up his position; he came home in January, 1778, but sailed again for America in April. His sorrowful wife and her two children accompanied him to Portsmouth, where she bade him farewell, and then returned sadly and alone to Culford.

The park at Culford was beautiful when Lady Cornwallis reached home, the trees were opening in their soft green and the birds were nesting in their branches, but the loveliness only increased her intense longing for her husband and the nightingale's song in the summer nights only sharpened her sadness. Not even her children could console her and her grief gradually assumed such proportions that she became seriously ill. Towards the end of the year her attendants and her doctors realised that her condition was dangerous and word was sent to Lord Cornwallis, who set sail for England at once, arriving home at the end of January, 1779. But he was too late, nothing could be done to save his wife, and she died on 13th February. It was learnt afterwards that Lady Cornwallis had confided in her maid that she was dying of a broken heart, and she requested that no stone should be carved in her memory, but only a thorn-tree planted, as near as possible to the vault where she lay at rest, a sign of the sorrow which killed her. The inscription on her coffin read "Jemima Countess Cornwallis, died February 13th, 1779, aged 31½ years". She must have been the saddest of the Ladies of Culford. A thorn-tree still grows near the Cornwallis vault on the north side of the Church, significant not only of Lady Jemima's sorrow, but of her husband's anguish at losing her.

Bereft as he was, Lord Cornwallis returned to America and commanded his Division until the disastrous defeat at York Town, Virginia in 1781, when he surrendered with all his men to General Washington.

Cornwallis was not blamed for this defeat, and five years later was appointed Governor-General and Commander-in-Chief in Bengal in succession to Warren Hastings. He fulfilled this task with great success, and stayed in India until 1793. Before he went out to Bengal he was made a Knight of the Garter, and on 17th February, 1787, he wrote thus to his only son Charles, Viscount Brome (now thirteen years old and at Eton),

My dearest Charles,

The intelligence packet arrived here on the 11th of this month, and to my great joy brought me your letter of the 14th of June. . . .I am a Knight and no Knight, for my Stars, Garters and Ribbons are all lost in Arabia, and some wild Arab is now making a figure with "Honi soit qui mal y pense" round his knee. I hope you have got enough French to construe that, but I own it is not a very easy sentence. If I continue to hear good accounts of you, I shall not cry after my stars and garters. . . .

Your most affectionate father,
Cornwallis.

Lord Cornwallis obviously missed the company of his children, particularly Viscount Brome, and he wrote to him frequently. James Cornwallis, the Earl's younger brother, now Bishop of Lichfield and Coventry,* was guardian to the boy during his father's absence, and also saw to the management of the estate at Culford.

It was during Lord Cornwallis's absence in India that Culford Hall was greatly altered in style. The first reference to this alteration which we have been able to find is in a letter written by Earl Cornwallis to his brother James, as follows:

Calcutta, Dec. 7. 1789,

Dear James,

I wrote to you so fully last month on all domestic concerns, that I shall only, for fear of accidents, briefly recapitulate that I leave it to your discretion, either to confine yourself to the repair, or to make alterations in Culford House, that at all events I wished it not to be inhabited the last year† and would give 200L to the Singletons for the hire of a house for that time . . . .I expressed my obligations to you for your attention to secure Stow, which is a most desirable object.

"The Singletons" were his daughter, the Lady Mary and her husband Captain Mark Singleton, of the Guards, a son of Sydenham Fowkes of West Stow Hall, who had made a runaway marriage in 1785.

A notice appeared in *The Bury and Norwich Post:*

Dec. 14. 1785.

A few days since was married, Capt. Singleton, of the Guards, to Lady Mary Cornwallis, daughter of the Right Hon. Earl Cornwallis of Culford, near this town.

---

*The Hon. James was also Dean of Durham; he it was, who, arriving at Durham in the summer of 1796, and discovering that the architect James Wyatt was about to pull down the Galilee Chapel in order to make a carriage road from the Castle to the West Door of the Cathedral, immediately stopped this plan from being carried out.

†The last year he expected to be in India.

And again:

Bury. Aug. 12, 1789.

Lord Cornwallis's return to this country is fixed for the summer of 1791, preparatory to which his family seat at Culford, near this town, is undergoing a thorough repair.

The reason for this repair, or alteration, is not known. The seventh Earl Cadogan has stated that he always understood that the original Elizabethan house was damaged by fire, whilst Lord Cornwallis was in India; this may have been so, it would certainly have provided a good reason for re-building, or extensive "repairs", but despite the most thorough and painstaking searching, no proof of this has been found. There was a fashion at that time for covering Elizabethan buildings with a facade of Georgian design, and it seems as though this might have been done at Culford.

In 1790 the Bishop of Lichfield wrote to his brother William, Admiral Cornwallis, ..."I hope to go to Culford next week, and expect to find great progress in the house. Palgrave was here the other day, I shewed him the plan of the house at Culford, of which he expressed great approbation. It will certainly be a most excellent house and I think the whole expense cannot exceed £5,000."

The alterations were carried out by the firm of de Carle, Stonemasons, who were closely related to the notable Norwich family of the same name; a certain Robert de Carle worked as a mason and architect in Bury St Edmunds between 1724 and 1796, and there is ample evidence in the de Carle Wages and Day Books held by the Record Office in Bury St Edmunds that this firm did the work:—

1794. Work done at Marquis Cornwallis acct. delivered to Mr. Wells.

	£	s	d
Ye measured work to ye House	1,513	10	4¾
Do.	54	5	8½
	1,567	16	1¼
Bill to ye Offices	284	17	7¾
Day Bill	162	4	10½
Total	£2,014	18	7½

This amount in all probability was not the whole expense, as there are numerous small items: "A mason 1 day fixing irons for the Gates to North and South Front . . . . 3/6.

To No. 32 stone posts with a mortice cut in each to fix an iron Railing round the Hall at 2/- . . . . £3 6 0"

etc. etc.

We are also told that "Cany and Walls laid ye Hall floor, and Dempster". This presumably is the stone-flagged floor of the Inner Stairway, one of the most beautiful parts of the building.

Whether this Robert de Carle was the architect for the rebuilding, as well as being in charge of the actual work, it is difficult to say. It has been said that Robert de Carle was the architect, but the style very much resembles the work of James Wyatt, the celebrated architect who was active at that time, and who was responsible for some of the work, and particularly the carvings and mouldings, at Heveningham Hall, Suffolk. The dome above the stairway of Culford Hall resembles the Cupola Room at Heaton Park, Manchester, also designed by Wyatt; and a later alteration to Culford was carried out by George Wyatt, a relative of James. On the other hand no reference to Culford has been traced in the records of Wyatt's work, and it is possible that de Carle was the architect and copied the work of more famous men. The grounds were laid out afresh by Humphrey Repton, and in his Report, still in existence, he states:—

> I had not the honour to be consulted before the stile of the old mansion had been altered, but as the *same outside walls remain,* it is evidence that the character of the house must nearly be what it was with respect to its size. . . ."*

Repton's comments support the theory that the walls of the red brick Elizabethan building still remain, covered by a façade of "white" Culford brick, made in the brick-yard where all the bricks used to be made — the brick, known as white, is actually a very pleasing shade of greyish fawn.

---

*The present Bursar of Culford School has had a portion of the wall uncovered which proves the author's theory that only a 'skin' of grey brick was fastened on; whether the red bricks immediately beneath are the originals or not, it is difficult to say.

The main entrance of the Elizabethan house was at the south front, but in this alteration a new entrance was made at the north front, as is shown in a vignette which Repton drew in his Report, and as may be seen from other illustrations of the period. This Georgian house still exists as the kernel, as it were, of the present Hall, of which more will be said later.

For his services as Governor-General of India, Earl Cornwallis was made a Marquis and the *Bury and Norwich Post* reported on 12th February, 1794:

> Few circumstances have ever given more general satisfaction to the inhabitants of this country, than the safe arrival of Marquis Cornwallis, after so long an absence; his private virtues are so well known to almost all ranks in this neighbourhood, that his first visit to Culford Hall (which elegant mansion during his absence has been completely new modelled) will be marked, we have no doubt, with those heart-felt congratulations so justly due to his exalted rank and character. The Marquis is now at his brother's house (The Bishop of Lichfield and Coventry) in Wimpole Street, Cavendish Square, where he arrived on Saturday morning; and we are happy to hear, in a good state of health.
>
> The news of the noble Marquis's arrival was most welcomely received on Thursday last at Eye, in this county, where it was celebrated by the firing of guns, ringing of bells etc., and in the evening the corporation and freemen were respectively entertained at the Town Hall and the White Lion.

and also,

Bury and Norwich Post, 5th March, 1794:

> Monday evening Marquis Cornwallis, accompanied by Lord Brome, Mark Singleton, Esq., and Lady Mary Singleton, arrived at Mr Edward's at Chesterfield Inn, at which place they slept the night, and yesterday morning set out for Culford Hall, near this town, where the noble Marquis and his family arrived yesterday to dinner, and we have great pleasure in saying, in a much better state of health than the public has reason to apprehend from recent accounts given in some newspapers. His Lordship's safe arrival in Suffolk after so long an absence, must diffuse general joy to the surrounding neighbourhood, as his many amiable qualities have long endeared him not only to his tenantry, but to all with whom he is either acquainted or connected.

Thus the noble Marquis returned to Culford, to find the Hall very different from the house he had known when he left for India in 1786.

Repton's plan was made and signed in 1791, and presumably most of the improvement was completed by the time Cornwallis came home. He was delighted with the comfort of his "new-modelled elegant mansion" and the beautifully laid out grounds, described thus by Humphrey Repton:—

> The house stands on the side of a hill gently sloping towards the South, but nearly one half of the natural depth of the valley has been destroyed to obtain an expanse of water, which in so flat a situation I think ought not to have been attempted. I am certain by proper management of the water the Hall would appear to stand on a sufficient emminence above it, and not so low as the present surface of the water seems to indicate. . . .

In his plan, one may see how the original lake, dug by Sir Nicholas Bacon's fifty men, which lay to the south-east of the old Elizabethan Hall between the grounds and Culford Village, was enlarged by digging away the ground between two small streams which ran away from the lake to the west, and directly in front of the Hall. The water flowed into the bed thus made, and so the lake in Culford Park as it is today was made. Repton also planted numerous new trees in the park forming long vistas, and, in addition, a "thickcover" by the village, where the old road from Bury used to run, so that the "noble family" residing in the mansion should not be offended by the sight of so many "cumbrous appendages" (villagers' cottages.) He also advised the building of "offices" next to the House for the use of the servants, and recommended that the kitchen gardens should be moved further to the east, away from the house.

The Marquis had brought back with him cannon which had been captured in India; these were used to make the iron structure of a bridge which was thrown across the lake, and the road over the bridge and across the Heath beyond to the Newmarket Lodge at the south-west of the Culford Estate became the main drive to the Hall. What a picturesque approach it must have been in the old coaching days. The track may still be followed, but the Newmarket Lodge is gone.

The villagers of Culford, who lived in the "cumbrous appendages" which were such an eye-sore to Humphrey Repton, served the Cornwallises of that generation as their forefathers had served the earlier family. Several references to the labouring men on the estate were found in the local papers of that time. One poor man's death is described thus:

Bury, May 10th, 1796.

On Thursday last as two labouring men were felling an oak tree at Culford, near this town, one of them (Henry Parnall) set his leg too near the tree, and received a wound from the axe of the other man, which divided the small bone and part of the large one a little below the knee. He continued in great pain about half an hour, when he died from loss of blood. The deceased was in the 77th year of his age.

There is also an entry on 21st August 1793, in the *Bury and Norwich Post:*

On Sunday morning last between one and two o'clock, as one of the carpenters employed at Culford Hall was returning home, he was stopped near the bridge which runs over the canal by two foot-pads, who robbed him of 8s. in silver, and after otherwise using him very ill, threw him into the water, from whence he had some difficulty in getting out.

Eight shillings probably represented a week's wages in those days.

The Marquis was tired of travelling and of being out of England, and hoped now to be able to live the life of a country gentleman. Whilst still in India, through the good offices of his brother James, Bishop of Lichfield, he had bought the estate of Little Saxham, possibly with the intention of eventually living there, but on reaching England and seeing the beauty of Culford he decided against Little Saxham, and was able to make an exchange for the estate of West Stow, which his brother had previously investigated. This was in the year 1795, a very hot summer, according to a letter of the Marquis:

Culford, 20th Sept. 1795.

Dear Ross,

The same dry and hot weather still persecutes us, and is equally hostile for shooting and to the turnips, and there never was a year so universally bad for partridges. . . .

In 1799 Lord Cornwallis further enlarged his estate by purchasing Wordwell from Lord Bristol, paying £33,000 for it, and thus enlarging his lands, comprising Ingham, Timworth, Culford, West Stow and Wordwell to 11,000 acres. His years of service to his country were bringing him wealth as well as distinction.

In the meantime, his son, Lord Brome, had married on the 17th April, 1797, Louisa, the fifth daughter of Alexander, Duke of Gordon, and he brought his bride to live at Culford. The Marquis, whilst being very fond of his new daughter-in-law, and later of her children, seemed to object to the gaiety and sociability of life at Culford, now that there was a new young Mistress. The house-parties of elegant young men and women, patched and powdered, dancing by night and filling the house with their laughter by day, irritated the tired soldier, and he wrote to his friend, Major-General Ross:

Culford, Aug. 20th, 1797.

. . . .The comfort of the country which I proposed to myself has suffered considerable abatement by the house having been completely full of young ladies in the highest spirits since Tuesday last. Thank God the Cadogans leave us tomorrow and the Townshends on Tuesday. . . .

(One of the ladies was Lady Emily Cadogan, nineteen years old at the time. She was later to become the grandmother of the fifth Earl Cadogan, who ultimately bought Culford Hall.)

So perhaps Lord Cornwallis did not take a great deal of persuading when he was requested by Pitt to go to Ireland as Viceroy and Commander-in-Chief. His quiet manner, tact and fairness in his dealings with the people gave great satisfaction, but this was not enough; again he was requested to serve, and was sent to Paris in 1801 to negotiate with Napoleon Bonaparte, which resulted in the Treaty of Amiens, signed in 1802.

Once again the Marquis returned to Culford, hoping at last to find rest and peace. The days passed pleasantly enough, as the life of a country gentleman should. He delighted in his son's company, and his son's children, all girls, and mentioned them often in his letters to friends; he seemed particularly concerned when "little Louisa has the whooping-cough". Letter-writing occupied a great deal of his time at this stage, often to eminent and leading political figures of the day, usually concerning politics, or the relationship of various members of the Cornwallis family to other important personages. In many letters the unbalanced state of mind of George III is referred to — always as "a certain Person"; whilst family affairs were regularly discussed with his brother James, who seems to have had the Marquis's best interests at heart.

About this time, the authorities of the County of Suffolk decided to apply to Parliament for permission to build a new road to Brandon which would be a continuation of the existing road from Bury St Edmunds, but instead of passing through Culford Village as it then stood, i.e. within the present park, it would keep straight on, passing between, on the left-hand (west) side, Home Field, and on the right, Twelve Acre Close, continuing between Parson's Gapp, on the left, and Scalding Lays (a large field of eighty-five acres) on the right. Thence it would turn to the north-west going across North Wood Penn, where it would turn due west and then north to Brandon. This plan was surveyed by John Griffin in 1802, and in 1804 permission was granted by Marquis Cornwallis for this new road to be built through his land, and the agreement was signed by "We, Sir F. G. Cullum and Sir Charles Davers, Baronets — two of His Majesty's justices of the Peace for the said County at a Special Session held at Culford in the Hundred of Blackbourn in the said County". (A copy of the draft is in the West Suffolk Record Office.)

So work was begun on the new road, and the building of it greatly affected the village of Culford, but not in the lifetime of the Marquis, for in 1804 he was again requested to go to India. He was feeling far from well at the time, and it was with a sad heart that he wrote to his friend, Lieut-General Ross:

Culford, Oct. 24 1804.

Dear Ross,

. . . .Nothing could induce me to return to India but the firm persuasion that it was the earnest wish of the Government and of the respectable part of the Directors.

If I stood on less independent ground, I might sacrifice my own good name without being able to render any essential service to my country.

It is a desperate act to embark for India at the age of sixty-six; prepared, however, as I am to forego all further comforts and gratifications in this world for the sake of my family, I cannot sacrifice my character and my honour.

Yours very sincerely,
Cornwallis.

The Marquis left England and his beloved family, in March, 1805, never to return, for he died in India in October of that same year.

Following is an account of his death, printed in the *Bury and Norwich Post,* 5th Februry, 1806.

Death of the Marquis Cornwallis.

On Tuesday the Medusa frigate arrived at Weymouth from Bengal, whence she sailed on the 3rd of November. . . . She brings intelligence of the death of Marquis Cornwallis, at Ghazeepore in the province of Benares, on the 5th of October. From the Calcutta Gazette Extraordinary:

Fort William, Oct. 12. 1805.

With sentiments of the deepest sorrow and regret, the Government announces the decease of the Most Honourable Charles Marquis Cornwallis, Knight of the Most Noble Order of the Garter, Governor General of the East India Company's Possessions, and Commander in Chief of His Majesty's and the Honourable Company's Land Forces in the East Indies.

In the first page of this paper are inserted the melancholy particulars of the death of the Most Noble Marquis Cornwallis, (as extracted from the Indian newspapers) of Culford and Brome Halls, both in Suffolk. —

A Nobleman highly distinguished and respected in this his native county, and whose absence therefrom at such an advanced age (however laudable the motive) was much regretted in this neighbourhood, where, probably, he might have continued in the enjoyment of health and life to a period more distant than that in which it terminated. His Lordship is succeeded in title and estates by his only son, Charles Lord Viscount Brome, now the Most Noble Marquis Cornwallis, by whose advancement to the Peerage there is a vacant seat in the representation of this County in Parliament.

And later: *Bury and Norwich Post,* 12th February 1806.

> The principal inhabitants and corporation of Eye, appeared in deep mourning on Sunday se'nnight as a mark of respect for the late noble Marquis Cornwallis, and walked in procession to Church, where the organ played that solemn anthem "The trumpet shall sound, and the dead shall be raised," which was very impressively sung by Mr J Clouting, organist. The tradesmen of this town, and his Lordship's tenantry in the neighbourhood, also paid a tribute to his memory by appearing in mourning on Sunday last, when the parish Church of Culford was hung with black. It is needless to say how much his Lordship's loss is lamented as a sincere friend, an excellent landlord, and a liberal benefactor to the poor in the vicinity of his hospitable mansions at Brome and Culford.

A monument was subsequently erected to the Marquis's memory in St Paul's Cathedral, and the original model of this, by Charles Rossi, can be seen in the Chapel of Audley End near Saffron Walden, which became the home, on her marriage, of the eldest daughter of the second Marquis Cornwallis, and was presented to her by Lady Mary Singleton, daughter of the first Marquis.

Shortly after the death of Marquis Cornwallis, his son, the second Marquis, had Culford Hall altered again. The house as it stood had a semi-circular entrance the curve of which was carried up to the roof; it was not very elegant, but George Wyatt removed the solid entrance and put in its place a semi-circular portico, which added to the dignity of the house. He also altered the slope of the roof in a way which revealed the line of the domed roof of the main staircase, and this, too, added greatly to the beauty of the outside of the Hall. An architect's elevation for this work, signed and dated by Wyatt (1806) is in Lord Cadogan's possession.

The actual building of the portico was carried out by the firm of de Carle, as may be seen in one of their Day Books:—

Aug. 15th 1807

Acct. for building of Portico at Culford

	£	s	d
Day Senr at Culford 7 days about ye Portico	1	4	6
Allowc.		3	0
His Son		5	0
	1	12	6
Girling at Culford 7 days abt. ye Portico		15	0
Day Senr about ye Portico at Culford 7 days	1	12	6
Expended for Beer and other expenses at Culford Portico	1	0	0

1808

Jan. ye 16

Day 5 Days at Culford about ye Paving at ye front of ye House North	1	5	0

March ye 12

Wegg 6¼ Days — two at Culford *fixing ye Library Chimney Piece	1	2	0

The result of these alterations was a very elegant small country house of beautiful proportions. It had twenty bedrooms, a library, boudoir and diningroom, a business room, kitchens below, and servants' quarters (Tudor brick may be seen in parts of the cellars beneath, dating back to the first, Elizabethan Hall), and a very fine stairway hall, with an excellent wrought-iron balustrade surmounted by a beautiful dome decorated in rich plaster work of fruits and sphinxes in the Adam style. The delicately moulded ceilings and door-casings of the various rooms were also in the Adam style, and to this day remain beautiful examples of chaste design, whilst the doors were all made from Spanish mahogany.

Lord Brome, now the second Marquis Cornwallis, was somewhat over-shadowed by the activities of his illustrious father, but according to the reports of the day, he was a very likeable and kindly man. He was educated at Eton, and was a Master of Arts

---

*"Ye Library Chimney Piece" is the one still in the library.

of St John's College, Cambridge when he was twenty-one. In the same year, 1795, he secured the seat in Parliament for Eye, Suffolk, the town which the Cornwallis heir had always represented, and was made M.P. for the County of Suffolk in 1802, a seat which he held until 1806, after which he sat in the House of Lords. He was described as "as much beloved as he was respected", and of "being held in great and deserved estimation". Unhappily, as with so many of the Cornwallis line, his life was short; he died on the 9th August, 1823, in Old Burlington Street, Middlesex, in his forty-ninth year. His widow, Louisa, Marchioness Cornwallis survived him for twenty-seven years, dying on the 5th December, 1850, aged seventy-three. Both are buried in Culford Church, where tablets have been placed on the west wall to their memory. Two of their daughters who died unmarried, Louisa and Elizabeth, are also buried in the Cornwallis vault.

So came to an end the Cornwallis line at Culford. The Marquis left no heir, and the Marquisate expired, the title passing to his Uncle James, the Bishop of Lichfield, who became the fourth Earl Cornwallis.

The year following the death of the Marquis, 1824, the estate was sold, and the Cornwallises walked at Culford no more. The eldest daughter, Jane, had married Lord Braybrooke of Audley End, Essex, and she took with her the family portraits which she inherited. There they may still be seen, amongst them the picture of Lady Jane Bacon as a young woman, silent reminders of the history of a noble family.

The New Village

THE years which followed the death of the second and last Marquis Cornwallis were in many ways uneventful so far as Culford Hall was concerned; but for the villagers great changes were taking place.

Mr Richard Benyon de Beauvoir of Englefield House in Berkshire, and High Sheriff for Berkshire in 1816, was the purchaser of the Culford Estate and entire parish of Culford, Ingham, Timworth, West Stow and Wordwell, in 1824 for £230,000; he was a very wealthy man, reputed to be worth over seven millions. He married Miss Elizabeth Sykes, only daughter of Francis Sykes, of Basildon Park, Berkshire. Originally his name was Richard Benyon, but in 1814 he was quite unexpectedly left a million pounds by the Rev. Peter de Beauvoir, no relation to him, and thereafter he was known as "Benyon de Beauvoir". It was during his time as Lord of the Manor that many changes were made at Culford. He did much to improve the grounds and make new roads, as is clearly seen from the correspondence of some of his employees to Mr Benyon, still in existence. These letters, mostly from Robert Todd who appears to have been the agent, and from William Armstrong, the head gardener, largely concern the day-to-day work on the estate when Mr Benyon was not in residence, and also give some interesting details concerning the domestic life of the workers.

Extract from letter of Robert Todd to Mr Benyon de Beauvoir, Culford, 8th April, 1825:

. . . . The cottages where Dixon did live are geting forward Cotterells will be fit to be inhabited within a few days, the hot house is nearly finished the bricklayers work is done and the carpenters nearly so.

They are now laying the foundation for the wall across the lower Garden and geting the materials to the field by the scotch Firs in readiness to begin those cottages. Sodens men are at work at the Stow pit and roads, have graveled chief part of the road from Flempton Bridge to Stow Churchyard. . . . . Armstrongs men are upon the coach road by the school he will discharge several on Saturday night. Poor old Phillip Mothersole your bricklayer at Culford is dead, his son is going on with the work as usual.

I remain Sir
Your Most Obt. and Humble Serv.
Robt. Todd.

P.S. Mr Nockolds I find is coming on Monday next.

Letter from Thos. Hubbard to Mr Benyon de Beauvoir, Hengrave Cottage, April 19th, 1825:

Dear Sir,

You are well aware that Mr and Mrs Armstrong have been living very uncomfortably for some time, I think it proper to acquaint you the waves of discord are at this time *rolling mountains* high. I have been applied to by both parties but chiefly by the woman (whom from my soul I pity) to remove her from the house in which she ought to have found comfort and peace, but instead thereof I fear she has experienced not only *insult* but blows. I think a separation is necessary to prevent *worse* consequences: before I proceed in the business I should feel particularly oblig'd by your advice.

We shall be most happy to hear a favourable account of Mrs Benyon's health to whom with Miss Benyon and yourself we beg our Compliments.

Remain Yours truly
Thos. Hubbard.

Extracts from letter of Robt. Todd, 6th May, 1825:

. . . . Soden has done the new Road to the Newmarket Lodge and all the others excepting that from Wordwell towards Elden* over the Heath, where all his men are now at work.

. . . .I have brought a pair of young Chesnut Horses such as I hope (after a little practise in harness) will please you in your Carriage they appear to be quiet and very good tempered. Mrs Forty is tolerably well.

---

*Elveden.

Ilsley tells me he mentioned in his letter to you all that was going on with the buildings.

> I am Sir
> Your Most Obt. and Humble Servt.
> Robt. Todd.

P.S. Armstrong and his wife are parted she left Culford last Tuesday, is in lodgings at Bury at present.

Extract from letter of Robert Todd to Mr Benyon de Beauvoir, Culford, 29th May, 1825:

. . . . It is said the navigation is likely to be stoped* about three weeks.

. . . . I think Sir you ought to see Culford now if you wish to see it in its beauty the white thorns in the Park are now in full blossom and looking very handsome.

> I am Sir
> Your Obt. and Humble Serv.
> Robt. Todd.

Extract from letter of Robt. Todd to Mr Benyon de Beauvoir, Culford, 27th July, 1825:

Sir,

Mrs Ling tells me she does not know how many of the *Boys* and how many of the *Girls* at the School you intend clothing but wishes to know as soon as possible the time being so near that you said they should have them Mrs Forty always used to cut out the Girls Clothes would you like her to do so this time, I have got 19 suits of the Boys Clothes sent to me.

. . . . The Cottage below Warners is slated and the inside work is getting forward the Cottage by the School is finished excepting laying two floors, Mr Normans Barn is finish'd and the other work is going on pretty fast so is Mr Harrisons likewise Mr Waltons old House is down and they are now laying the foundation for the new one.

---

*This would refer to the River Lark which runs through Westston, then a navigable river. In the *Bury and Norwich Post* for April 22nd 1806, a notice was inserted to the effect that navigation would be "stopped from the 12th May next, to repair the sluices in the Fulling Mill, in the Parish of Westston".

Soden is going on with the Coach Roads in the Park. Ilsley says he set the workmen on at Downham.

I am Sir
Your Most Obt. and Humble Servt.
Robt. Todd

Extract from letter of William Armstrong to Mr Benyon de Beauvoir, Culford Hall, 16th October, 1825:

. . . . The Road opposite Warners, is cut through to the Bridges but no Gravel on it, as yet. Sir, Thos. Ayres desires me, to tell you, that there is 40 Teal on the Water, that is likely to remain, and do well at present.

Your Most Obedient and very Humble Servant
William Armstrong.

Extract from letter of Robert Todd to Mr Benyon de Beauvoir, Culford, November 27th, 1825:

Sir,

I have received four cases of wine and have put them into the store cellar where they now remain the same as they came.

. . . . Ilsley is home from Downham but we have not arranged about the Blacksmiths shop nor the things which you mentioned at the Hall but Ilsley will attend to them the begining of this week and write you the particulars both as to Downham and Culford. I hope Sir Mrs Benyon is quite recovered from her fall, and that she may enjoy her Christmas with you in Berks.

I remain Sir
Your Most Obt. and Humble Servt.
Robt. Todd.

P.S. Soden is got through with one side the road by Warners and began picking up the road from Ayers lodge to the Hall next week will begin forming the road in the Park from Stow.

Between the time when Humphrey Repton re-planned the grounds and park for the Marquis Cornwallis, until 1834, when the estate was surveyed by Lenny and Croft, of Bury St Edmunds, the face of Culford Village had changed beyond all recognition. It may be remembered that Repton had advised the planting of trees "in a thick cover", to hide the "mean hovels of the village" (then built close to the Church) from the sight of the Hall. But with the building of the new road of 1804, the new Culford village began to rise by the side of it; gradually the old houses were demolished, until only the Rectory, near the Church, a small Dame's School (that for which Mr Benyon supplied the children's clothes), opposite the Church, and the farm buildings were left, and we must not forget the stables built by the first Earl Cornwallis, which still stood. In the place of the old village, trees were planted by the side of the old road, eventually forming the avenue of fine Wellingtonia lining the drive up to the Church from the main Park Gates in the new Culford Village, for the Park was by this time enclosed, and a Lodge was built at the Culford Gates, which still stands. Opposite the main Culford gate, the *White Hart Inn* was built, now a residence known as Benyon Lodge. Remains of the old village are still buried in the land behind these trees, and recently a quantity of old glass and brick of considerable age was unearthed there. The fields through which the new road ran also received attention from the planners, and a new large kitchen-garden was made there, with greenhouses, gardener's house, and carpenter's yard (all still standing), and running along from the stables, past the kitchen-gardens and the carpenter's yard was made a road called "Butcher's Lane", which joined the main road in Culford village, and which became the chief road used by tradesmen to the Hall.

Whether Richard Benyon de Beauvoir tired of East Anglia, or never had any great interest in Culford we do not know, but in 1839 his nephew, the Rev. Edward Richard Benyon was instituted Rector of Culford St Mary, and shortly afterwards Mr Richard Benyon de Beauvoir presented him with the estate for his life.

The Rev. Edward Richard Benyon was in a unique position as Rector of the Parish, and the owner of the Estate. He was, more-over, a landlord with the interests of his parish very much at heart, and spent considerable sums in building, and in improving the grounds. The head gardener at the time of E. R. Benyon was Mr Peter Grieve, who was responsible for the planting of the yew hedges, which were at one time one of the chief attractions of the gardens. Peter Grieve excelled also in the cultivation of geraniums, and reared several famous ones whilst at Culford, amongst them "Culford Rose", and "E. R. Benyon". He also published in 1868 a small book entitled *Variegated Zonal Pelargoniums;* he was evidently a gardener of some distinction.

The Rev. Mr Benyon used some of his money for the re-building of the Church, as a tablet near the South Door records:

This Church, together with the Chancel and vestry, were wholly re-built and the tower (which formerly was brick) heightened and covered with Bath stone by the Rev. Edward Richard Benyon, the proprietor of the Culford estate, and rector of the parish, 1857.

The date above the South Porch on the outside of the Church, however, is given as 1856. At the same time he built a new school in the village, near the *White Hart Inn,* and on the site of the old Dame's School, opposite the Church, he built a row of four widows' cottages, which are still used. Many of the flint cottages in the village were doubtless built by him as well, since they figure on maps of the period. Then, in the year 1865, he built an entirely new Church at Culford Heath. This hamlet, some three miles to the north of Culford, past the prehistoric tumulus known as the Hill of Health, is a very isolated place of a very few cottages. At that time the Rector of Culford drove to Culford Heath every alternate Sunday and held a service in the little school for the benefit of the parishioners, more numerous in those days, so the Rev. E. R. Benyon decided it would be very much better to have a church out there. Accordingly he built a large Victorian edifice, but the population of Culford Heath decreased rather than increased, and the large Church was a source of embarrassment to subsequent Culford rectors, who could not afford to keep a curate especially to be in charge of St Peter at Culford Heath, nor did the tiny congregation warrant the service of such a curate; eventually the Church fell into disuse, until at this date services are never held in it at all.

Mr Benyon was an amateur archaeologist, and associated himself with much local history and excavation, particularly with the unearthing of the Anglo-Saxon cemetery on West Stow Heath in 1851. In the museum in Bury St Edmunds known as Moyes's Hall is a stone coffin discovered in the Anglo-Saxon cemetery by Mr Benyon and presented by him to the museum.

E. R. Benyon had no children, and when in 1876 his wife died, he placed two stained glass windows in the chancel to her memory, representing Faith and Hope. The friends of this good lady placed a third window, Charity, on the south wall of the chancel, bearing the following inscription:

> To the Glory of God
> and in Memory of Jane Benyon
> By her sincerely attached Friends.

Mr Benyon did not long survive his wife; he was buried at Culford on 13th July, 1883, he and his wife resting side by side near the south porch of the church, which he undoubtedly had greatly loved. After his death the estate passed to a relative, Mr Richard Benyon Berens, the eldest son of Richard Beauvoir Berens. He seems to have left no trace at all of his ownership of Culford, and in 1889 he sold the manor and the entire estate to the fifth Earl Cadogan. Thereupon the Culford scene was once again changed, and the great days of the Cadogans began, with a splendour and magnificence not seen for many a year.

SERVING with the great Duke of Marlborough at Blenheim was a young General of thirty-two years, named William Cadogan. His ancestors in mediaeval times lived in Wales, and spelt their name "Cadwgan", but in the early seventeenth century a certain Major William Cadogan, the grandfather of William who fought at Blenheim, and who had been born at Cardiff on the 5th February, 1601, became Lord Lieutenant of Ireland, and made his home at Liscartan, Co. Meath. He died at Dublin in 1661, and it was at Liscartan that his grandson William, the eldest son of his only son Henry, was born in 1672. William Cadogan was noticed as a promising soldier very early in his career by Marlborough, and became one of his ablest staff officers, serving at Ramillies in 1706, Oudenarde 1708, and Malplaquet 1709, as well as at Blenheim. Whilst stationed at the Hague, where Marlborough's headquarters were established, the young Cadogan married Margaretta Munter, the daughter of William Munter, a counsellor at the Court of Holland, who bore him two daughters, Sarah and Margaretta. From 1705-1716 he was M.P. for Woodstock and was created Baron Cadogan of Reading on the 21st June 1716, and raised to an Earldom in 1718. He died at Kensington Gravel Pits on the 17th July, 1726, and was buried privately in Henry VII's Chapel in Westminster Abbey; as he left no male issue he was succeeded as Baron Cadogan of Oakley, by his brother Charles, who also served under Marlborough in some of the later campaigns. This Cadogan married in 1717, Elizabeth, one of the daughters of the famous Physician, Sir Hans Sloane, the owner of much property in Chelsea, which resulted in the estate of Chelsea becoming vested in the Cadogans; he was also the donor of large sums of money for the founding of the British Museum and was made a Trustee thereof, which position has been regularly held by the succeeding Cadogan heirs. Charles, Lord Cadogan, lived to be eighty-five, and died in September, 1776 at his house in Bruton Street. He was succeeded by his only son, Charles Sloane, who was created Viscount Chelsea and Earl Cadogan on the 27th December, 1800. This Lord Cadogan was the first of the family who appears to have been in any way connected with Suffolk; an entry is recorded in the *Bury and Norwich Post* of the 19th January, 1789 that, "At the quarter sessions held here on Monday last, the Right. Hon. Lord Cadogan appeared on the Bench, and qualified himself to act as a Justice of the Peace for this county." Again, on the 9th of June, 1802, the following notice appeared in the *Bury and Norwich Post:*

> Wednesday was married at St George's Hanover Square, London, the Hon. Mr Wellesley (brother of the Marquis) to Lady E. Cadogan, daughter to the Earl of Cadogan, of Santon Downham, in this county.

Lady Emily was one of the young ladies staying at Culford in August, 1797, about whose high spirits Marquis Cornwallis ruefully complained. Her husband was a clergyman, the Hon. and Rev. G. V. Wellesley, brother of the Duke of Wellington. He was a Canon of Durham Cathedral for twenty-one years, and lived in a house built into the Old Monks' Dormitory there. There is a memorial to him in the Transept of the Nine Altars, Durham Cathedral, where he is buried near two of his grandchildren. The third daughter of Lady Emily Cadogan and the Rev. G. V. Wellesley was Mary Sarah, who on the 13th July, 1836, married in Durham Cathedral her cousin, Henry Charles, fourth Earl Cadogan, who was born in South Audley Street, on the 15th February, 1812, and was the grandson of Charles Sloane, the second Earl, who lived at Santon Downham, near Brandon, Suffolk, where he is buried and where there is a memorial plaque in his memory. On 12th May, 1840, at Durham, Lady Mary the Countess Cadogan, gave birth to a son, George Henry, who, on the death of his father, on the 8th June, 1873, became the fifth Earl Cadogan. He it was who became in 1889 the owner of Culford Hall and the entire estate of nearly 11,000 acres. He was educated at Christ Church, Oxford, and when he was twenty-five, on the 16th May, 1865, he married at Durham, Lady Beatrix Jane Craven, the fourth daughter of the second Earl of Craven, by Emily Mary, daughter of James Walter Grimston, Earl of Verulam. The Cadogans had quite a long connection with the Cathedral of the north before they came to Culford.

George Henry, the fifth Earl Cadogan, lived in Chelsea House, Cadogan Place, London, as well as renting various country properties. He held numerous important positions during his lifetime and was a friend of Queen Victoria, who often sought his advice. He was made under-secretary for War in 1875, an office which he held for three years, and was Lord Privy Seal from 1886-92. He became Lord Lieutenant of Ireland from 1895-1902, the First Mayor of the Borough of Chelsea, and a Hereditary Trustee of the British Museum. He was also the father of seven sons and two daughters; the third son became the sixth Earl, and the youngest, Alexander (1884-1968) was Great Britain's first representative to the United Nations, and Chairman of the Governing Body of the B.B.C.

All their family were born before his Lordship bought Culford Hall, in 1888-9. It was said at the time, and quoted in both *Vanity Fair* (November, 1888) and *Truth,* (January, 1889) that the "ugly brick house" (the lovely Georgian House built of Culford brick) was to be replaced by "an immense Elizabethan House". How taste had changed in a hundred years. *Vanity Fair* also stated that "an interesting house exists on the estate, it having been the residence of the Duke of Brandon and the Dowager Queen of France, one of whose children born there was the mother of Lady Jane Grey." This is an error; the residence referred to is West Stow Hall, built by Sir John Croftes, who was of the household of Mary, sister of Henry VIII, the Dowager Queen of France and the wife of Charles Brandon, Duke of Suffolk. In compliment to his royal mistress Sir John Croftes placed her arms over the gate of West Stow Hall, and this has given rise to the mistaken idea that the Duchess of Suffolk lived there from time to time. In actual fact she lived at Westhorpe and died there in 1533; her body was buried in the Abbey of Bury St Edmunds, and at the Dissolution was removed to St Mary's Church nearby. The child supposedly born in a house on Culford estate, was her daughter Frances, born at Hatfield on the 16th of July, 1517, who became the mother of the ill-fated Lady Jane Grey.

But although Lord Cadogan did not build an "immense Elizabethan House", he nevertheless made great and vast alterations to Culford Hall as it then stood, completely altering the style of the Georgian house, and, many would say, spoiling it. A diagram shows how he achieved this, by building on an entirely new front and almost encircling the small Cornwallis home. This work to the design of an architect called William Young was begun soon after his Lordship bought the estate, the bricks for the purpose being made in the brickyard, as had been those for the Cornwallis house. At the same time very fine new stables were built from "red Culford brick" away from the house to the north, situated by the side of what used to be the main road through the park. These red bricks were also used to build a Post Office, several new houses in the village for estate workers, a new laundry by the road called "Butcher's Lane", and eventually a new school and a large Village Hall.

During this period of alteration to his new country house, converting it from a modest twenty-bedroomed Hall to a Mansion of fifty bedrooms, Earl Cadogan was in Ireland as Lord Lieutenant, and in the Athenaeum in Bury St Edmunds is a bust of Queen Victoria presented to Lord and Lady Cadogan by Her Majesty, as a mark of her esteem for the way in which they fulfilled this task. Returning to Culford, Lord Cadogan set about putting his estate in order, ready for the entertaining of Royalty. The gardens, already laid out with great beauty, were tended with much care, and in the glasshouses peaches, grapes and nectarines flourished; water melons were cultivated, roses grew in profusion, and fountains played on the well-kept gravel paths. It is said that there were about twenty gardeners employed to keep all in perfect order, several blacksmiths for the shoeing of the horses and the making of farming and gardening implements, wheelwrights, carpenters, and an expert cabinet-maker who looked after the furniture of the Hall and even made some of it. Nor did His Lordship neglect his employees; several references may be seen in the local press of the time to entertainments arranged for their benefit and meals provided in the grounds on their behalf. In return they gave him unstinted service. In fact the people who worked for Lord Cadogan were exceptional – loyal, devoted, and entirely uncomplaining. In those days there were no buses at all, and if they wished to go into Bury St Edmunds the villagers of Culford had to walk there and back, or ride an ancient bicycle. Apart from the few new houses built by his Lordship, and the new School and Village Hall, the village was much the same in size as it had been for nearly a century, and under Lord Cadogan's rule no public house was allowed; the *Cadogan Arms* was at Ingham, but at Culford the only place to get a drink was in the "Workmen's Room"; known locally as "The Room", it still survives. Nor was there any shop until an old lady named Mrs Crack started to make toffee which she sold from her little sitting-room to the children on their way to school. Mrs Crack's shop was the forerunner of succeeding shops which have developed, attached to the Post-Office, and present day children still love to call in to spend their "new pence" on their way to school.

There are people living in Culford still who well remember the visit in December, 1904, of King Edward VII and Queen Alexandra. His Majesty had already stood as sponsor, along with the future George V, to the Earl's grandson, Edward George John Humphrey, the son of Viscount Chelsea, the Cadogan heir, and his wife the Hon. Mildred Cecelia Stuart, daughter of the first Baron Alington. It was therefore as a friend of the family that he came to visit Lord and Lady Cadogan, and was drawn by the estate workers in his carriage up the drive planted with Wellingtonias, the drive which had once been the village road, up which Edward I cantered on horseback six hundred years before.

There was very much to show the King. Firstly, the grounds with the beautiful gardens, and the magnificent wrought-iron gates leading from one part of the grounds to another — those at the entrance to the pleasure gardens were supposed to have belonged at one time to Anne Boleyn; the great acreage of woodland planted with fir trees and beech every year, giving employment to many people; the flocks of sheep which were meeting with such success at the Royal Show, the Norfolk and Suffolk Shows and others; and the well-managed farm with the herds of Jersey cows.

Looking at the mansion from the north front shining in its newness, with a stone balustrade surrounding the roof ornamented by stone vase finials, and surmounted by the copper cupola, did the King, one wonders, approve of the extensive alterations? It would seem that he may not have visited Lord Cadogan had the Hall remained its former size; and it is known that the King's Equerry insisted that suitable alterations be made in the plumbing before the Royal party arrived.

Entering by a new square stone portico (George Wyatt's semicircular one having been pulled down in the extensions) the visitors walked into what was called the Inner Hall, a large room, about fifty feet long, which had been made by knocking down the entrance of the old Cornwallis Hall and building out a huge extension. This made an imposing kind of lounge-hall. It was fashionable at this period of building to copy earlier styles of design, and the architect, for his new hall and for the corridor leading from it to two drawing-rooms, seems to have copied the more elaborate styles of the mid-eighteenth century, rather than the restrained late-Georgian or Regency style of the Cornwallis house. The ceiling of the Inner Hall is decorated with plaster-work in a bold geometrical design, there is an ornate painted frieze with classical figures, and above each doorway is an embossed pediment, crowned with an Earl's Coronet, and the cipher of the Cadogans (✕ — Chelsea, Cadogan). On each door-post, his Lordship had placed carved female figures, and under-neath each figure, a small plaster figure of a bird, or a lyre, a dog, or an artist's palette, a globe, a stook of corn, a bunch of grapes, the implements of husbandry, presumably symbolic of the life lived at Culford. In contrast to the Inner Hall, and the long corridor, both painted white, the two drawing-rooms opening off the corridor were both richly decorated with gold after the manner of the work of William Kent who designed Holkham Hall in Norfolk, the door of the "red-room" being a double door of the same period. The tapestry in the red drawing room and the extremely ornate gilding have stood the test of sun and time remarkably well, the gilding is still well-preserved, but the crimson silk tapestry is beginning now to wear badly. The smaller drawing-room had an ormolu-mounted marble fireplace, and the gilding here was less heavy than in the red drawing-room; the gilded wall-candelabra and the gilt musical instruments are still well-preserved.

Returning to the Inner Hall from the Corridor, two fireplaces were to be seen, one with a design of cherubs' heads and Prince of Wales' feathers, and the other a much more ornate example of sienna marble, built into an alcove, which was supported by two female figures — these were subsequently removed and Ionic columns substituted, which were considered more suitable when Culford Hall eventually housed a boys' school! Incidentally, the columns are probably more in keeping with the rest of the decoration at that end of the lounge-hall, which appears to be the original 1790 style, the restrained moulding above the doors and below the cornices of the ceiling corresponding exactly with the doors and cornice mouldings of the early part of the mansion.

Passing out of the Inner Hall, the Royal party came to the Georgian part of the building, the house built for Marquis Cornwallis; it is still very beautiful, with a quiet, chaste dignity, and a serenity in keeping with the Suffolk countryside. Here may still be seen the beautiful Adam-style ceilings, the delicately carved architraves of the doorways, the elegant stone stairway with the wrought-iron balustrade and the dome with its geometrical carvings.

Hanging on the wall of this stairway is a very fine portrait of William, the first Earl Cadogan, who fought at Blenheim with Marlborough. The portrait is reproduced in Sir Winston Churchill's *Life of Marlborough*.

The rooms leading from the stairway hall were the Library (part of the original building) and the Boudoir — later the study. The Library is still as it was planned, and is still used as a library. It has an elegant ceiling, a delicate Adam fireplace, and the classical mouldings surrounding the bookshelves correspond to those in the stairway hall. It is 49 feet long. The Boudoir was a particularly fine room with lovely windows overlooking the lake and the terrace at the south front; it connected, by a double door, with the (then) dining-room, later Lady Cadogan's Boudoir; this also was a beautiful room, its walls hung with blue tapestry and the fireplace decorated with exquisite pink Wedgwood panels. (The fireplace is now in the drawing-room of the house built for the first Headmaster of Culford School, near to the Hall.)

On the terrace at the south front of the house a portico had been built out, supported by heavy pillars, which quite altered the façade of the house at that side and made the dining room and boudoir appear dark. Subsequently, many years later, the pillars supporting the portico were thought to be unsafe, and they and the portico were taken down again; so that at the present time that part of the Hall appears as it did in the Cornwallis days, excepting that in the pediment surmounting the façade the Cadogan coat-of-arms has been inscribed, bearing their motto "Qui invidet minor est", "He who envies is the inferior".

Later, Lord Cadogan added a new dining-room and still-room to the Hall, with bedrooms above, building them directly in front of the servants' quarters which had been built for Lord Cornwallis thus depriving his employees of light and air, and shutting out their lovely view of the south front. But these things were accepted without question in Victorian and Edwardian times, and the people who worked in the Hall, or on the estate, seem to have been very happy with their lot. The dining-room, of oak, with an ornately-carved dado, and a heavily encrusted plaster ceiling and frieze in a floral design, is 44 feet long by 30 feet wide; in it is a picture showing the Battle of Malplaquet. The story goes that the young General Cadogan whilst reconnoitring before the battle sighted the position of the French cannon, and dropped his glove on the ground as an indication of where to bring up the English guns. The picture shows Cadogan and Marlborough riding up to the scene of battle on the following day, with the glove lying in the foreground. This picture also was reproduced in Sir Winston Churchill's work on Marlborough; it is the property of Earl Cadogan as is the painting of the first Earl Cadogan.

Electric light had been installed on the estate for the visit of the King, there being "over a thousand lights in the mansion alone". Lord Cadogan was described in *Country Life* (10th February, 1906) as "this enlightened landlord", and there can be no doubt that he ran the estate in a most business-like way; the farms flourished, the flocks of Suffolk and Southdown sheep increased and multiplied, and over all was a great sense of well-being, culminating in this high light of social life, the visit of the King and Queen. Many are the tales told of the dinner-parties, the balls, and the excellent shooting enjoyed by the house-party; there is a photograph still in existence, taken by the Bury St Edmunds photographer Mr H. I. Jarman, of all the members of the house with their Royal guests and others, seated in front of the stable gateway, showing the clock above, which was erected in 1892 by the firm who made the clock at Victoria Station, Lillett and Johnson of Croydon. But for all the gaiety and merriment, each day began with prayer. The late Canon Woodard wrote in 1957 that as Chaplain to the fifth Earl it was one of his duties to breakfast daily at the Hall, after prayers for family, guests and household.

To mark their visit, the King and Queen each planted a mulberry tree on the lawn at the south front, between the two cedar trees planted many years before, possibly by Humphrey Repton, maybe by Thomas Wright, fifty years earlier. The mulberry trees bear much fruit every year.

During the years which followed many important visitors came to stay at Culford as the guests of Lord Cadogan, and the King honoured him more than once in the shooting season. The late Mr H. I. Jarman related to the author how he once came to Culford to take a photograph of a shooting party, when whom should he see but Queen Alexandra, mounted, side-saddle, with a groom holding the bridle, in front of the portico at the north front. She smiled graciously at him, and she looked so lovely he wished he had been able to paint her, but was too shy and tongue-tied to ask permission even to take her photograph.

These visitors must all, as does every visitor to Culford, have stood on the terrace at the south front, looking at the movingly beautiful scene before them; at Repton's simple yet elegantly planned grounds, at the lake, which the Earl had caused to be entirely cleaned and cleared of weeds, revealing a fine expanse of clear water, and at the new stone bridge which he had made in the place of the Marquis Cornwallis's iron bridge (the iron support is supposed to be the original); perhaps they strolled on the lawns and listened to the fountains playing, and watched the setting sun light up the sky behind Nicholas Bacon's plane tree in the west, or walked amongst the acres of parkland, or crossed the bridge and wandered over the heath, still as it was in Prehistoric times.

Presiding over this peaceful splendour was a very gracious lady, Beatrix Craven, Countess Cadogan; her mother was Emily Mary, the daughter of James Walter Grimston, Earl of Verulam, who was a direct descendant of Sir Harbottle Grimston and his first wife Mary Croke. Sir Harbottle's second wife was Anne, the widow of Sir Thomas Meautys, and she was the daughter of Sir Nathaniel Bacon and Jane Lady Bacon; their little daughter, who died in May 1657, when she was four years old, is the child seated on the lap of Lady Bacon in the monument in the chancel of Culford Church, and who is buried near the altar.

So the wheel had come round full circle, as it were, and the gracious lady of the Manor of Culford had direct connections with those who had lived here in Jacobean times. Thus it seems most fitting that when she died aged sixty-three on the 9th February, 1907, she should be buried in a vault in Culford Church. There her husband erected a new north aisle in her memory, with a small tasteful chapel at the east end of it, where her tomb stands.

The Earl and Countess Cadogan's eldest child died in 1878, a boy aged twelve. This must have been a great grief to them.

The second son of the marriage, Henry Arthur, Viscount Chelsea, born in 1868, married on the 30th April 1892, the Hon. Mildred Cecilia Harriet Stuart, the daughter of the first Baron Alington. Viscount Chelsea died when he was forty, on the 2nd July, 1908. His widow married again, nearly two years later, but a few months after her marriage to the Hon. Sir Kedworth Lambton, son of the Earl of Durham, the son of her first husband, Edward George John Humphrey, died on the 2nd June, 1910. So it was that the third son of the fifth Earl Cadogan, Gerald Oakley, born on 28th May, 1869, was his successor when he died on the 6th March, 1915. His Lordship had married again in 1911 his cousin, Countess Adele Polagi, but he was buried at Culford in the vault with his first wife. There is no tablet to commemorate him. Gerald Oakley, Viscount Chelsea, was forty-six when he became the sixth Earl Cadogan. He married on the 7th June, 1911, which was almost a week before the Coronation of George V. Viscount Chelsea's bride was Lilian Eleanora Marie, the only daughter of George Coxon of Cheltenham; she had three children, William Gerald Charles, born on 13th February, 1914, Beatrix Lilian Ethel, born 12th May, 1912 and Alexandra Mary, born on the 10th March, 1920, the same year in which her aunt, Alexandra Mary, after whom she was named, and for whom Queen Alexandra had been sponsor, was married to the tenth Duke of Marlborough, thus renewing the alliance between the Marlboroughs and the Cadogans.

Under the new Earl, the estate was managed in much the same way as it had been in the fifth Earl's time. Huge parties and dinners were given in the Hall, and the grounds were regularly thrown open to the public in aid of charity, the local hospital particularly benefitting in this way. Girl Guides were a cause in which the new Countess was interested, and rallies were often held in the park, a notable occasion being the visit of the Princess Royal, daughter of George V, who was then known as Princess Mary, for a Rally of Girl Guides in July 1926. The work of the estate was continued much as before, the park and gardens being well-tended, and the trees watched with particular care. The work of the carpenter's yard was still carried on, the plant for the making of electricity still used to light the estate and to pump electrically the water into the water-tower from the great well which had supplied Culford with water for years, and which is still the only source of supply. His Lordship was very interested in all wild life, particularly in birds, and he made a list of over ninety birds which he had watched in the park. He used to sit at his desk in the study, the window of which overlooked the lake, and by his side a pair of field glasses always stood ready to spot any strange or unknown object on the water, which might be a bird new or rare in these parts. In those days, the reeds growing in the lake were always cut and used for thatching, and there were men working in Culford and West Stow not long ago who could well remember stepping onto the frozen lake to cut the reeds.

But those days of splendour, of great entertaining and excellent estate management came to an end all too soon. In 1933 the sixth Earl died, and because of death duties, the size of the mansion, and the difficulty of maintaining sufficient staff to run such a place, the new Lord decided to leave. Born on the 13th February, 1914 he spent his childhood at Culford and was educated at Eton and Sandhurst. He served in the war of 1939-45, and was awarded the Military Cross. He has three daughters, and one son, Viscount Chelsea. Lord Cadogan still shows 'an interest in the place which was his home, and is a Governor of Culford School. He was also the last Mayor of Chelsea before it became part of the Lieutenancy of Greater London, his grandfather having been the first Mayor.

Over 5,000 acres of the estate south of the Thetford Chase were sold to the Forestry Commission and planted by them in Commemoration of King George V's Jubilee of 1935. This afforestation was named the King's Forest, and a column of flint was placed at the entrance to it along the Brandon Road north of Culford, recording the fact.

To the great sorrow of the estate workers, who had been really happy and contented under the Cadogan rule, the rest of the estate was split up and sold to various buyers, whilst the mansion of Culford Hall, after remaining empty for nearly two years, was eventually purchased by the Methodist Education Committee, prompted by the Headmaster of the East Anglian School for Boys in Bury St Edmunds, Dr John W. Skinner, who was strongly supported in this scheme by the Educational Secretary, Dr Herbert Brook Workman. To these far-sighted men must go the credit for the fact that Culford School came into being in 1935. The history of the School has been written by better-informed and far abler writers; we are concerned only with the story of Culford until that day, and it is nearly told, but before closing let us look for a moment at Culford Church again, where so many memories still linger.

The Church of St. Mary, Culford

CULFORD Church stands at the left-hand of the drive from the main gates of the Park. It is a Victorian building of stone and flint built by the Rev. E. R. Benyon in 1857 on the foundations of an earlier church. There is a tablet to this effect on the wall over the south door inside the Church. But we have seen as we have followed the history of the Cootes, the Bacons, and the Cornwallis family that a church existed at Culford years ago, in the days when the Abbot of St Edmundsbury owned the domain, although there is very little to show when this early church was built. It is known that Sir Stephen Fox, the father-in-law of the third Lord Cornwallis, the notorious Cornwallis who was at one time indicted for murder, re-built the church in either 1673, the year in which his daughter Elizabeth married Lord Cornwallis, or 1679, the year in which she died. Years later, it was discovered when the Rev. E. R. Benyon re-built the 17th century church, that there had been wall paintings in the *original* church; these paintings had been on the splays of two narrow round-headed lights at the east end, which had been blocked up, possibly when Sir Stephen Fox built the second church, if second it was. The subject of the murals was a martyrdom by fire, possibly St Lawrence; there were three medallions in each window, one on either side and one in the vault above. The fact that the windows were splayed, points to their being of twelfth or thirteenth century design, and the fact that they were round-headed seems to prove that these windows had been late Norman. A further point in our investigations is the fact mentioned earlier in this short work, that Abbot Anselm, Abbot of St Edmundsbury from 1119-1148, gave some lands in Hausted for the advowson of the Churches of Culford and Barton, which in turn were to pay yearly, 40s. to the altar of St Edmunds. So that it is possible that the first church we had at Culford was built in the first half of the twelfth century, and almost certainly it was this church which still stood when the Bacons came to Culford. It was here they were buried and many of the Cornwallis family too, and when re-building later took place their tombs and memorials were undisturbed.

The best approach to the church is along the avenue of clipped limes leading to the west door, a lovely entrance in summer when the limes are in full leaf, and quite dramatic in winter, when the stars may be seen shining above the bare branches of the tall trees growing near the church door.

As one enters the West Porch one notices first the memorial on the north wall to Sir Nathaniel Bacon, who died on 1st July, 1627, aged forty-two, Lady Jane's second husband, and the seventh son of Sir Nicholas Bacon who built the first Culford Hall. The memorial is in the form of a bust, with an artist's palette and brushes at the corners reminding us of his skill as a painter and with the Bacons' arms above. It is the work of Thomas Stanton, and bears the inscription:—

Viator Specta
Nathanielis Baconii ad balneum regale
Torquati Equitis
Effigies
Haec est

Quen quum usus et observatio in stirpium historia sapientissimum fecerant eundem, eu mirum, im iisdem penecillo exprimen — dis sola natura docuit arte naturam vincere sat debes oculis, Vale.

On the south wall is the memorial to the second Lord Cornwallis and his Lady, Margaret Playsted; she died in March 1668, he in April 1673. The memorial is in the form of a long double tablet placed on the wall, but only the right-hand side, recording the death of the Lady Margaret, was filled in, evidently by her husband; the names of her eleven children are placed there, the five who died in their mother's lifetime, and the six who survived her.

On the floor of the porch are slabs covering several members of the Cornwallis family; there is Charles Lord Cornwallis, the fourth Lord, who died in January, 1721, and his Lady, Charlott, who died in August, 1725. There are two children of Charles the second Lord, Nathaniel who died on the 30th September, 1656, aged two years seven months, and Elizabeth who died, aged four years and three months, on 14th April, 1664. In the north corner of the porch, almost hidden by a pillar which was built above it when the Church was rebuilt, lies the body of little Jane Meautys, the only daughter of Sir Thomas Meautys and his wife the Lady

Anne, the daughter of Lady Jane Bacon. This child died on the "7 day of Aprill, 1652"; the inscription on the slabstone where she is buried reads:

Jane Meautys, only daughter and heire of
Sir Thomas Meautys.
The joye of vertue who'd not one teare shed
Here on a dusty pillow layes her head
Death's blow wch had most cause in doubte did bring
Earthe to lament, or heaven for joye to singe.
Earthe is depriv'd of a bright pearle of grace
A starr of glorry shines upon heaven's face.

She was ten years old.

At the west end of the nave are the slabs in the floor where two more of the second Lord's children lie, Frederick and Anne, who died within ten days of each other in July, 1655. These children, Frederick, Anne, Nathaniel Cornwallis and Jane Meautys, together with Anne Grimston and Jane Bacon, are all depicted with Lady Jane Bacon, in the memorial to her in the church.

A tablet on the south side of the west wall records the death of the second Marquis Cornwallis:

In memory of Charles
Second and last Marquis Cornwallis
Who died on the 9th August, 1823
In the 49th year of his age.
This tablet is erected
By his widow and children
To record the irreparable loss
Which they have sustained.

On the north side of the west wall is a tablet;

Sacred
To the memory of
Louisa Marchioness Cornwallis
4th daughter of Alexander, 4th Duke of Gordon.

She was born 27th December 1776 and died 5th December 1850, aged seventy-three. In compliance with her wish expressed in her will she had sepulture in the family vault in this Church near the remains of her beloved husband.

There is also a tablet to the memory of two of the Marquis's daughters, Louisa, the second daughter, who died in 1872, aged seventy-one, and Elizabeth, the youngest daughter, who died in 1874, aged sixty-seven. Both are buried in the Cornwallis vault.

Originally the Church consisted of a single aisle and chancel, but when his wife died in February, 1907, the fifth Earl Cadogan pulled down the north wall and built the north aisle with the chapel containing her tomb. In doing so, some delicate wall paintings in the old north wall were destroyed; but a certain Rev. C. W. Jones made some copies of these pictures, which are quite delightful and, it is thought, depict the story of St Barbara. In all probability they date from the earliest church.

The Chancel, as built by the Rev. E. R. Benyon, has a wooden hammer-beam roof with carved angel finials; according to the Register, in the time of the Rev. Nicholas Wakeham the chancel twice received considerable attention e.g.,

1. In the year 1758 the chancel of Culford was repaired and tiled by J. Claxton, carpenter, and – Steel, bricklayer of Bury – N.W.

2. In the year 1766, the roof of the chancel was entirely taken down, and repaired with all new material, N.W.

On the step of the Chancel is a small slab, which states:

Here lieth the body of Martin Norridge who departed this life the .... (date worn away) of March, 1983:–

This was the Martin Norridge, who preached the sermon at the "funerall" of Lady Jane Bacon, and who was minister to the Parish for some thirty-seven years. It seems fitting that his bones should rest near to those whom he served so well and for so long; for built into the wall on the north side of the chancel, not many feet away from where Mr Norridge lies, is the memorial to Jane, Lady Bacon. This interesting monument shows her seated in a chair with a little girl on her lap, Anna (or Anne) Grimston, her daughter's child by her second marriage; at her right hand the figure of her own daughter Jane who died in infancy, and her granddaughter Jane Meautys; at her left-hand her three great-grandchildren. Anne, Frederick and Nathaniel Cornwallis. At her feet lies the recumbent effigy of Sir Nicholas Bacon, her son who died in 1660, a year after his mother. Many writers have made the mistake of thinking that this figure of a man lying at the foot of the statue represented Lady Jane's husband, Sir Nathaniel Bacon; but Sir Nathaniel's memorial, erected by Lady Jane, takes the form of the bust on the north wall of the West Porch which has already been mentioned. Her first husband, Sir William Cornwallis, who died in 1611, the father of her son Sir Frederick Cornwallis who became the first Baron Cornwallis of Eye, was buried in the Paris Church of Oakley, near Brome, where Lady Jane (Cornwallis as she then was) erected a marble altar-tomb as his memorial, bearing the following inscription:

> After he had lost his son, he turned once more to matrimony and made a most successful marriage with Jane Meautys. She was the daughter of one of the noble squires who attended Queen Elizabeth, Hercutio Meautys, who was the son of the Knight Peter Meautys, in the County of Essex and of Phillippa Coke, the daughter of Squire Richard Coke, of Giddy Hall, in the County of Essex.

> Jane Meautys bore him an only son, Frederick Cornwallis of Broome, Knight and Baronet, but she did not think it enough as a devoted mother to leave her son, a living reminder of his father. At her own expense she arranged for this monument to be set up, the tribute, assuredly, of a fond wife to her loving husband.

Moving to the north aisle, erected, as a tablet on the wall shows, to the Glory of God, and in memory of Beatrix Jane Craven, Countess Cadogan, by her husband the fifth Earl Cadogan in 1907, the chief object of interest is of course the chapel containing Lady Cadogan's tomb showing her lying full length at rest on top of the marble with her name and the dates of her birth, 8th August, 1894, and her death, 9th February, 1907. Round the tomb are inscribed the words "The fruit of the spirit is Love, Joy, Peace, Long-Suffering, Gentleness, Goodness, Faith, Meekness, Temperance". The arms of Cadogan are carved on the pall and their motto at Lady Cadogan's feet "Qui invidet minor est", whilst cherubs and angels traced in the stone on the wall behind her support a scroll bearing the words "Faith, Charity and Hope."

People who can remember Countess Cadogan say that this effigy is an extremely good likeness of her; it was executed by Countess Fiodore Gleichen, who was a grand-daughter of Queen Victoria's half-sister, and a well-known artist in Victorian days. A bust of the Queen, for which Queen Victoria actually sat, in the South African War Memorial at Eton College, is an example of the Countess's work.

The sons of Lady Cadogan placed a stained glass window in the north wall of the chapel, in memory of their mother.

In the new north aisle, west of the chapel containing Lady Cadogan's tomb, are two more windows, one to the memory of Albert Edward George Henry, Viscount Chelsea, the eldest child of Lord and Lady Cadogan, who died aged twelve on the 2nd August, 1878, and the other in memory of Henry Arthur, Viscount Chelsea, their second son, who died aged forty on the 2nd July, 1908; whilst on the wall is a tablet "In memory of their beloved nurse Elizabeth Henstridge. This tablet is erected by William Edward and Alexander Cadogan, as a token of their Gratitude and Affection, 1912. Rest in the Lord."

The East Window, representing the Crucifixion, was placed there in memory of the fifth Earl's daughter, Emily Julia, Lady Lurgen, who died on the 12th December 1919, aged thirty-eight. She is buried in the Cadogan vault in the Church.

The window over the west door is the oldest part of the Church. It is composed of many small panes of glass, depicting the arms of Coote: Argent, a chevron, between three cootes, sable; of Bacon: Gules, on a chief argent two mullets pierced sable; of Meautys: Azure an unicorn salient Erminois, armed or; and Cornwallis: sable; guttee d'eau on a fess, argent, three cornish choughs, proper.

The Cootes occupied Culford in the fifteenth and sixteenth centuries, the Bacons in the sixteenth and early seventeenth centuries, the Cornwallis's from the seventeenth century onwards, whilst the Meautys arms are in honour of Lady Jane Bacon's ancestors. Heraldry was much used in the fifteenth century in stained glass windows, which points to the fact that this window was placed there in the time of the Cootes, and that the Bacons and the Cornwallis family incorporated their arms in the seventeenth century. In the lower right-hand side of the window is a piece of vivid blue glass, unconnected with the rest, which is possibly the remains of a thirteenth century window.

The bell which summons parishioners to Church at Culford was made by Thomas Newman in 1704, bearing the inscription:

Thomas Newman made mee 1704
Earl Cadogan K.G. had me recast 1906.
Restored G. J. Vale Richardson Bury St Edmunds, 1892.

Thomas Newman was born at Haddenham in 1682, and set up a foundry at Bury St Edmunds in 1735, but eventually moved to Norwich. According to Dr Raven, the Author of *Suffolk Church Bells,* his bells were "remarkable for their inability to make themselves heard among their fellows." Since there is only one bell at Culford, there is no such difficulty here, and many have responded to its chime on Sunday mornings, passing through the Churchyard where many Culford parishioners lie, amongst them, Thomas Ayers, who is buried near the South Porch:

Thomas Ayers, 1870 aged 87.
In friendship steady, in his dealings just,
He lived respected and lamented died.
His greatest pleasure to discharge his trust,
And punctuality his only pride.

And James Ling, buried to the north of the Church.

James Ling, Died at Culford January 3rd, 1888, aged 100 years.
Worn out and weary, left alone
Friends of my youth had long been gone,
When death so kindly called me home,
God's will be done.

Also in the churchyard is the tomb of Peter Grieve, famous gardener at Culford, and his wife; and next to them the tomb of their son. The inscription on Peter Grieve's tomb reads:

Peter Grieve
For 33 years gardener to the Rev. E. R. Benyon of Culford.
Born at Allanton near Berwick on Tweed 16th Dec. 1811.
Died at Bury St Edmunds 26th September, 1895.

The Rev. E. R. Benyon and his wife lie at the west of the South Porch, and a little further off is the tomb of Dr Workman, and his wife, bearing the inscription:

In memory of Herbert Brook Workman D.Lit., D.D.
Methodist Minister.
President of the Wesleyan Conference 1930.
Principal of Westminster College, 1903-1920.
A founder of Culford, East Anglian and Hunmanby Schools.
2 Nov. 1862 – 26 Aug. 1951.

Dr John W. Skinner, the late Headmaster of Culford School, was cremated when he died on 1st April 1955 and his ashes were scattered in Culford Churchyard and the Park; whilst at the north side of the church is the grave of young Viscount Chelsea, the grandson of the fifth Earl, who died on the 2nd June, 1910.

We are fortunate in having a complete list of Incumbents of the Church from 1319, as follows:

1319	Roger de Saxham.
1324	Joseph de la Snore.
1324	Roger de Bernyngham.
1367	Robert de John.
1368	Joseph de Donyngton.
1369	William Lovetoft.
1415	Joseph Leder.
1452	Joseph Bennish.
1452	Richard Morgan.
1454	William Stoke.
1459	Richard Fest.
1473	Joseph Stevenson.
1524	Roger Fyneux.
1524	Joseph Balkey.
1546	Joseph Turnour.
1555	Thomas Lynne.
1560	Robert Allen.
1573	William Browne.
1604	William Knight.
1623	James Warwell.
1646	Martin Norridge.
1683	James Davies.
1709	Charles Carter.
1755	Nicholas Wakenham.
1790	Henry Wakeham.
1839	Edward Richard Benyon.
1883	John Joseph Roumieu.
1902	James Mahomed.
1926	J. S. Vallalley.
1932	W. S. Andrew.
1935	J. H. Sandford.
1958	F. Fuller.
1961	H. S. Godwin.

The dates are all of the year in which the Rector was instituted. Many Rectors stayed at Culford a long time; James Davies twenty-six years, Charles Carter forty-four years, Martin Norridge thirty-seven years, and Henry Wakeham forty-nine years. The living seems to have supported two parsons at times, a rector and curate, as for instance William Browne, who was inducted in 1573, and who was obviously living in Culford whilst Robert Allen was the "Minister", since there are several entries in the Parish Register of the births and deaths of "Mr Browne's" children, yet he never signed the Register himself. The entry of his own burial was made on the 22nd of December, 1606. The next Rector, Rev. William Knight, was buried in the Church, and his burial is also recorded in the Register: "Mr William Knight, parson of Culford, was buried upon the 10th day of February, 1623". But the only ones to whom there is any memorial, are Martin Norridge, whose resting place is marked by the stone slab on the chancel step, and the Rev. E. R. Benyon, whose tombstone is in the churchyard.

James Warwell and Martin Norridge were the respective parsons throughout the time at Culford of Lady Jane Bacon, and she remembered each of them in her will.

James Davies, instituted Rector in 1683, left a note in the Register to the effect that he, at his own expense, built the small barn with the stabling at the parsonage, in 1690", "which thing may the all-powerful God prosper to his and his successors' use". In those days, the parsonage stood close to the church and was still standing in the nineteenth century, as may be seen on maps of the period, but there has been no rectory at Culford for many years.

The Culford Parish Register dates back to the year 1560, when Robert Allen was the Rector. Although this was during the Lordship of the Coote family, there is no entry in the register of the birth or death of any Coote. The Register begins:—

> The Register of Culford in Parchment for Mariages, Baptizings and Burialls testifyed to be a true copy out of the former record in paper to the yeare of our Lord, 1597, and thenceforth according to ye constitution ecclesiasticall in this case by her Mtie authorised and comanded.

The first entry is:

> An'o Dom: Robert Drewe was baptised the 4th daie of December. 1560.

Robert was a very popular name for boys, as also Richard and Thomas, though one baby boy born in October 1574, was given the elegant name of Cyprian; he was the son of Richard Lakeie, but his brother, born two years later in 1576, was named plain George! Alice, spelt "Alise", Margaret, Elizabeth, "Jone", Marie and Catharin were common amongst girls and women. One girl was given the name "Triphena", she was the daughter of Richard Miller and was born in 1607, she "marryed" John Soare on the 21st September, 1629.

The first entry under "mariages" reads:

Richard Dunch and Alse (Alice) Coppin were married the 4th daie of November An'o 1560.

but in the next paragraph, "Burialls", poor Alise Dunch is entered as having been "buried ye 6 of Aprill 1562". Richard, fickle man, did not spend much time in grief, for

Richard Dunch and Margaret Calowe were married the 19 daie of August An'o 1562.

And the following August,

Thomas Dunche ye sonne of Richard Dunche was baptized the 6 daie of August, An'o Dom: 1563.

No further entry is made of the Dunches, so whether they left the district, or whether their deaths were never recorded, we do not know.

There were a great number of "Mulleys" living around these parts in the sixteenth and seventeenth centuries as also "Cocksedges", "Mowers", "Bishops", "Lakisses", "Larlinges", and "Nunns"; there were also a few "Cakebreads".

Until the year 1607 the witnesses to the Parson's signature at the foot of each page of the Register, being unable to read or write, signed with their mark. The first Churchwarden to sign so, was Thomas Best, who made his mark so — "X". When he died himself in February, 1604 he was recorded as "Father Best", and of his wife, who died the year previously, it is recorded "Mother Beste was buried the 6 day of April, 1603".

A little further in the Register is the entry of the death of Mr John Fenne, who was buried on 27th August, 1653. He it was of whom Nathaniel Bacon wrote to his wife "Bid John Fenn to send my coulleurs as soon as possible". And when the eighteenth century is reached we read of the burial of "John King Footman to Ld. Cornwallis, Sept. 5, 1769;" footman, that is, to the young second Earl, who later became the famous Marquis. . . .

There are several entries in the Register of the reading of "briefs", which were letters from the Bishop ordering a collection to be made in the Parish for some good cause:

Oct. 7th 1711 Collected in ye Parish ye sum of four shillings and one penny to a Brief for Long Melford Church in ye County of Suffolk 00:04-1.

and:

Collected towards ye Relief of ye inhabitants of North-Maston in ye County of Bucks, The summ of two shillings and a penny ye present 6th of April, 1707.

also:

Read at ye same time but collected nothing towards ye Relief of ye inhabitants of Towester in ye County of Northampton.

This page of Briefs, numbering about fifty in all, many of them to aid a Church damaged by fire, was signed "Wm. Chambers Curat ibm." It is amusing to read how many times the poor curate "read but collected nothing"; the inhabitants of Culford evidently had fixed ideas as to what they would support.

The church plate is not extensive, but what there is is good. There is a small modern chalice and paten, and a silver alms dish inscribed "In loving memory of Beatrix Cadogan, Presented by Mary Currie". The important pieces, however, are a chalice with lid and matching paten of heavy silver, each piece beautifully inscribed "This plate was given by the Rt. Honble. Charles Lord Cornwallis Baron Eye at Christmas 1713 to Culford Church". This is the fourth Lord Cornwallis buried in the West Porch of Culford Church, who died in January, 1720, the grandfather of the first Marquis for whom the Georgian Culford Hall was built.

There is also a very well-preserved Elizabethan Book of Homilies of 1563:

The Seconde Tome of Homelyes, of such matters as were promysed in the former part of Homelyes, set out by the Authorities of the Quenes Majestie:

1563.

The Table of Homelyes ensuying
For repayryng and kepyng cleane the Churche.
Agaynst gluttony and dronkennes.
Agaynst excesse of Apparell.
Of the State of Matrimonie.
Agaynst Ydlenesse
Of Almes dedes
An Information for them which take offence at certayne places
  of holye Scripture.

Conclusion

WHERE once the ostlers groomed his Lordship's horses, now the courtyard throngs with boys and masters moving to their lessons; where the Earl's laundry dealt with the linen for the Hall, now the sick are tended; and where once the graceful broughams wheeled up to the door at the north front, or in an earlier day the coach drew up from over the Cornwallis bridge to the sound of the horn, now the School bus grinds up the gravel to deposit or collect its passengers, according to the time of day. But had Culford Hall not become a School, it might have fallen into the ruin and decay which has been the fate of so many of our glorious country homes. As it is, many hundreds of boys have made this place their home for the greater part of every year, and though many of the once lovely rooms are now classrooms, much of the beauty of the building still remains; they can watch the swans nesting on the lake in spring, and see the Canada geese floating on the water; they can see the trees opening in their delicate greens in April, and watch them change to copper and crimson in October; the nightingale still sings in the beeches in the soft May nights, and Humphrey Repton's garden is a haven of tranquillity.

To see this garden by moonlight is perhaps the most magical touch of all; and if one walks alone, across the south front, one may hear as one passes the dining-room windows a dry soughing and crackling, like the sound of a sigh or the fall of footsteps on gravel. Could it be the little children of Nathaniel Bacon and Lady Jane, as they ran playing together? Or Lady Jane herself, pacing in lonely solitude after Nathaniel and little Jane had died,— or perhaps it may be the sighing of Marquis Cornwallis before he left his beloved Culford, never to return.

Of course it is none of these things, it is only the crackling of the large dry leaves of the late-flowering magnolia which Lord Cadogan had planted outside the dining-room; but by moonlight it is easy enough to imagine that the spirits of those who once lived here still hover over the brooding Hall.

Opposite the Mansion, at the north, a new building has been built for the furtherance of Science, in memory of Dr J. W. Skinner, on the walls of which is chiselled in brick the school motto, "Viriliter Agite Estote Fortes" — "Quit you like men, be strong". On the pediment above the façade of the Cornwallis building the Cadogans carved in stone their coat of arms with their motto, "Qui invidet minor est" — "He who envies is the inferior". But perhaps the most moving inscription of all is one, almost unnoticed, placed above the entrance to the kitchen garden, where once roses grew in profusion and little fountains played on the gravel drives. This tablet was erected by Beatrix Craven Countess Cadogan, mother of seven sons, whose final resting-place was Culford Church: she it was who had the water-lilies planted in the lake, and the snowdrops under the cedar-tree on the south front, and she it was who placed above the garden door this quotation:—

"Who loves a garden
Still his Eden keeps".

Time changes many things, and the face of the Culford of which we have written is no exception to this rule; but surely those who enter the many new buildings which are rising by the side of the old may learn something of the inheritance which is theirs, and find, as have so many before them, their Eden in this beautiful place.

Bibliography

E. Ekwal, Concise Oxford Dictionary of Place-names, Oxford, 1951.

Anglo-Saxon Charter, Augustus II, 84, British Museum.

Doomsday Book, ii, 364, 366b.

Patent Rolls, 2 Edward III, pt. ii, 23b.

Proceedings of the West Suffolk Institute of Archaeology, Vol. I. C. H. Hartshorne.

A. Page, *A Supplement to "The Suffolk Traveller"*, Ipswich, 1844.

W. G. Clarke, *In Breckland Wilds*, second edition, Cambridge, 1937.

O. Cook, *Breckland*, London, 1956.

Suffolk Green Books, Vol. 2, Nos. IX and X. Subsidy Lists, 1327 and 1524.

Culford Parish Register, 1560 et seq.

State Papers, 31 Henry VIII.

Verulam MSS., The Lord Keeper's Account, 20 Jan. 28 Elizabeth I, Folio 157.

R. Reyce, *The Breviary of Suffolk*, 1618.

F. de La Rochefoucauld, *A Frenchman in England*, 1784, translated by S. C. Roberts, Cambridge, 1933.

W. A. Copinger, *The County of Suffolk*, 5 vols., London, 1904.

The Visitations of Suffolk, 1561, 1577 and 1612. Edited by W. C. Metcalfe, Exeter, 1882.

The Private Correspondence of Jane, Lady Cornwallis; 1613-1644. Edited by Lord Braybrooke, London, 1842.

The Progresses of James I, Vol. 3, edited by J. Nichols from Birch's MS., British Museum, 4173.

D. Lloyd, *Memoirs 1637 to 1666*, London, 1668.

V. B. Redstone, *Memorials of Old Suffolk*, London, 1908.

State Papers Domestic, 1675. Public Record Office.

Proceedings of the West Suffolk Institute of Archaeology. Paper by A. Fea. 1937.

Cornwallis Papers. Elveden Hall.

R. Furneaux, *Tried by their Peers*, London, 1959.

Sun Life Assurance Policy No. 178559, 21st October, 1760.

Historical MSS. Commission, Vol. 6. 1909.

G. F. M. Cornwallis-West, *The Life and Letters of Admiral Cornwallis*, London, 1927.

Burke's Peerage.

West Suffolk Record Office Papers. Bury St Edmunds.

Bury and Norwich Post. 1700-1926.

The Correspondence of Charles, 1st Marquis Cornwallis. Edited C. Ross, 3 vols., London, 1859.

The Benyon Letters. Berkshire Record Office, Reading.

Vanity Fair, November, 1888.

Truth, January, 1889.

Dictionary of National Biography, Oxford, 1921-22.

W. L. S. Churchill, *Marlborough*. 4 vols. London, 1933-38.

Country Life, February, 1906.

Proceedings of the Society of Antiquaries, London. Paper by S. Tymms, 1856.

J. J. Raven, *Church Bells of Suffolk*, London, 1890.

Acknowledgements

My thanks are due to many people who have helped me in the preparation of this short work: to Lord Cadogan for his kindness in allowing me to have photographs made of the engravings in his possession of the first Culford Hall and the Cornwallis conversion thereof, for lending me his copy of the plan showing the alterations made by his grandfather, the fifth Earl, and for his permission to include the photographs of the two Cadogan paintings hanging in Culford Hall; to Lord Iveagh for his very kind permission to quote from Lady Jane Bacon's will in his collection of Cornwallis papers; to the West Suffolk County Achivist, Mr M. P. Statham and his one-time assistant Mr A. Allan, for freedom of access to information in the Record Office in Bury St Edmunds and for their personal help; to Mr W. J. Smith, the County Archivist of the Royal County of Berkshire, for obtaining copies of the Benyon letters from which I quote; to Mr W. Appell, the former editor of the *Bury Free Press,* for his generous permission to consult old copies of the *Bury and Norwich Post;* to the former Rector of Culford, the late Rev. J. H. Sandford, for his gift of Copinger's *Manors of Suffolk;* to Canon F. Fuller for his copy of a translation of one of the Verulam manuscripts and for the photograph of the self-portrait of Sir Nathaniel Bacon; to Mr W. E. M. Smith of Culford School who translated the Latin inscription on the tomb of Sir William Cornwallis at Brome, near Eye in Suffolk; to Mr G. Barber who, with the kind permission of the Rev. H. S. Godwin, photographed the monument of Lady Jane Bacon in Culford Church; and I am much indebted to my husband for his great help generally and to him and my sons for reading the manuscript, checking data and showing continued interest in the writing of this History of Culford.